The
Attraction
Distraction

Why the Law of Attraction ISN'T Working for You

and How to Get Results FINALLY!

Sonia M. Miller, BBA, MSW

ALMA
PUBLISHING

Dallas, Oregon

The Attraction Distraction: Why the Law of Attraction ISN'T
Working for You and How to Get Results FINALLY!
by Sonia M. Miller, BBA, MSW

ISBN-13: 978-0-9796745-3-2
First Edition: May 2008

Published by:
ALMA PUBLISHING

www.successforthesoul.com

Cover photography © Amanda Rohde
Cover art by Amy Dent Beebe
Cover design by Tony Stubbs

Printed in the United States of America

Table of Contents

THE MYSTIC'S FORMULA – STEP IV
Welcome It into Your Life

IN THE END

For
all the other
drops of water
in the ocean

Acknowledgements

They say it takes a village to raise a child. Well, after the journey I've traveled, I'm quite certain the same is true for the birthing of a book. From teachers who have generously imparted their wisdom, to family who have graced me with saintly patience, to friends who have cheered me on, to colleagues who have collaborated, and to all the clients who have shared their hearts and souls with such trust and courage...there are more to thank than I could ever recognize here.

That being said, I will not let this reality prevent me from attempting to acknowledge the many midwives (and "midhusbands") who lovingly, gently and sometimes firmly coaxed this book, my labor of love, into being.

To my husband who, after asking me if I wanted his honest opinion of my first writing attempts, blessed me with his best impersonation of a reader retching from nauseated boredom: thank you for loving me enough to be honest and remind me to "just write the way I speak."

To my early reviewers, Chris Miller, Cheryl Wenzel, Debbie Seys, Stephanie Fish, Don Seth, Rev. Harry Morgan Moses, Rev. David Alexander, Mary Hammond, Howard Brockman, Suzanne Blake, and Jennifer Steinman: thank you for taking the time to digest my book even in its roughest form and reflect back the insights that helped me chip away at my insecurities to reveal the truth of what I was trying to accomplish.

To my friends Annie Carofanello, Kristin Maze, JoEllen Charon, Stacey Lindsay, and Lora Cross: thank you for your ceaseless encouragement and for never once (after how many years?) getting sick of me talking about this book (at least you never said so).

To my proofreaders, Naomi Mahoney, Geralyn Pezanoski, Julie Domes, Carol DeJong, Stacey Lindsay and Lora Cross: thank you for your continuous encouragement and for lending your eagle eyes to soothe my perfectionist's paranoia.

To Tony Stubbs, my editor, book coach and publishing teacher: thank you for all the technical issues that you handled so beautifully with seemingly effortless ease, but moreover thank you for helping me to get out of my own way so that this book would finally become a reality!

And my family: thank you for living this life with me. You continuously help me to become all that I hope to be.

Introduction

In the year 2002, after almost twenty years of study, practice and experimentation regarding all things related to conscious creation, energy, and metaphysics, I set out to write a book with two goals in mind: 1) I wanted to write the book I wished I'd had along my journey – a book that would address the misinterpretations, distortions, unanswered questions and information gaps that often left me confused and frustrated.

2) I also wanted to contribute to making metaphysics mainstream. I wanted to help awaken *more* people to the higher truth of who we are: infinitely powerful co-creators. And, I wanted to do this not only for the peace and well-being it means for individuals, but for the inevitable ripple effect it can have on our world. At the time, concepts such as The Law of Attraction, visualization, affirmations, and the idea that we create our own reality were still considered fringe topics at best and ridiculous New Age woo-woo at worst.

It turned out that my voice was part of a growing chorus. Other messengers had similar goals. In 2004, the movie *What the Bleep Do We Know!?* was received with respectable acclaim. Through interviews with scientists, drama and animation, it delivered the compelling, entertaining and scientifically supported argument that we create our realities with our consciousness. At the same time, all sorts of books were coming onto the scene attempting to teach laypeople about quantum physics and the notion that reality is not what we thought it was. Then in February 2007, Oprah Winfrey delivered the movie *The Secret* to her national television audience. Viewers responded with such enthusiasm that a follow-up segment was quickly broadcast. In short order the movie and book became outrageous bestsellers; "The Law of Attraction" was being discussed over coffee and at the office water cooler, and a spirited dialogue, both inspiring and controversial, swept across national airwaves.

On the one hand, I was thrilled. I thought, "It's happening! It's really happening! People are waking up to higher truth! People are becoming willing to relinquish the idea that they are powerless amidst the greater forces of circumstance, our religions, our politics, our planet, or our universe. And it isn't just a few small pockets of people here and there who believe this. People are waking up on a mass level." My dream was being realized. Metaphysics was becoming mainstream.

On the other hand I wondered, "Well, now that more resources and teachers are becoming available, is there even a need for my book?" So, I watched and I listened. As the storm died down and the dust settled, I felt for a pulse. Slowly, but surely the beat and rhythm emerged. Now more than ever, people had questions. Now more than ever, seekers were inspired, but also frustrated by the unfulfilled promise of the Law of Attraction. Amidst stories of dreams realized, miracles manifested and desires fulfilled, many were left asking, "Why isn't this working for me?" "What am I doing wrong?" "Did I let myself get suckered in by a bunch of media hype?"

With this newfound perspective, the purpose of my book came into greater focus. There is indeed an array of educational material available for those who want to learn about the Law of Attraction. However, there is still a significant void when it comes to understanding what it really takes to access this potent and life-changing body of knowledge.

Within these pages, I hope to shed light on those subtle nuances and advanced principles which make all the difference. In this book, you will find a clear and simple overview of the Law of Attraction, what it is and how it works. But, beyond that, the majority of this book is designed to help you *get out of your own way so as to experience concrete results in your life!* Additionally, you'll get insight into the much bigger picture. Many people are drawn to these metaphysical principles because of the promise they offer for the manifestation of personal goals and dreams. However, the Law of Attraction can be about so much more. By opening up to a broader perspective, you'll discover that your goals and dreams are in fact a vehicle for spiritual development. The Law of Attraction can be the doorway that leads you to the higher truth of who you are!

With my sincerest wishes for a joyful, glorious life...

Choose Your Reality!™

Sonia M. Miller

1

The Opportunity

"Success is not to be pursued,
it is to be attracted by the person you become."

— Jim Rohn
motivational speaker, philosopher

This book is a manual for making your dreams come true. It is a compilation of everything I've learned manifesting my dreams, as a life coach working with clients pursuing their own dreams, and through the eclectic training I've received from all the different teachers life has sent my way.

I suppose the very personal force that has driven my life's work and consequently the writing of this book is that my history includes a long chapter of my life where I felt imprisoned by fear. Some of my earliest memories are those of being afraid. I was afraid I wasn't good enough; I was afraid of making mistakes; I was afraid of what people thought of me; I was afraid of disappointing people; when things didn't go as they should, I feared the worst. I worried all the time.

Although my inner world was one of constant worry and extreme caution, the outer image of my life portrayed a pretty, intelligent, smiling girl with a certain amount of privilege and plenty of opportunity. I got good grades. I did as I was told. My family was intact and involved in the community. I was well-mannered and always followed the rules. And despite my constant apprehension, I was a decent achiever.

What began as a childhood fear of chaos and a hypersensitivity to people's feelings, turned into the adult desire to control everything just so I could feel safe ... and so I controlled what I could. Instead of following my creative callings in college, I pursued a business degree because it would be safe and I was virtually guaranteed a financially secure job. If I let my walls down long enough to let a guy ask me out, I'd date only the ones with whom I could feel in control. Either they were emotionally or geographically unavailable, eliminating the terrifying threat of intimacy, or I felt superior to them so they could never really win my heart. I could never let myself feel anything; that would be way too messy and out of control. So I became the classic bulimic, stuffing a volcano of emotions down with food, while attempting to control weight gain through self-loathing purge episodes. Of course; all of this was shamefully private.

To the outside world, everything looked just fine. I was in control but in my inner world, I lived behind bars. I was the outsider looking in. I watched people engage with life. They had passions. They knew who they were and what they wanted. They were a part of the human race. These people were obviously comfortable in their own skins. They had a sense of humor about themselves. They were relaxed, spontaneous and *free!* I felt as if I were trapped in a bad dream, wanting to wake up yet unable to do so.

But somehow, despite the powerlessness I felt, there was a little flame of desire within me that never died. I'm convinced now that it was in allowing my *desire to live* that the Universe sent me the inspiration, teachers, resources and life conditions that would help me wake up and break free. And so I did. Upon graduating from college, which represented the final to-do on my dutiful-daughter checklist of responsibilities, I finally asked myself, "What do you want to be when you grow up, Sonia?" I had no idea whatsoever, but I finally had permission to ask. And so my journey began.

My "prison break-out" took about seven years. There were defining moments that marked the beginning of what I consider my awakening, as well as the final feeling of liberation. Over the course of many years, I was guided from one teacher or healer to the next. When I felt done with one, the next one would appear. But my liberation was only the beginning. Once I was free, my hunger for creative self-expression expanded even more!

Throughout this journey, I have worked with therapists, self-empowerment gurus, relationship coaches, energy healers and personal achievement teachers. I've done workshops and seminars, read countless books and filled as many journals. I discovered who I was. I joined the human race! I discovered my passions, set goals, achieved them, and fell in love with life and myself. The experience of liberation and authentic self-expression was, and has been, so indescribably life-affirming that it's all I've wanted to do ever since.

And so, the writing of this book is an expression of this passion. Nothing touches me more deeply than seeing the human spirit shine. There is nothing more fulfilling to me than watching those who have dared to dream embark on the journey of discovering their soul's truth, to become who they truly are fully expressed. Additionally, I certainly would have benefited from having had a "how to" manual on my journey. Everything I learned came from gathering bits and pieces from many different places. I figured if I could offer one solid resource for people wanting to create a life of personal fulfillment and success, now *that* would be something. And so, here is my best effort in that direction.

This book is about much more than mere achievement. Achievement can be about accumulating trophies, literal or figurative, that collect dust on your shelf, leaving you wondering, "Is that it?" This book instead is about *success for the soul*. It is about *using* your desires as a vehicle for spiritual development. It is about the deeply fulfilling and enriching journey of discovering the truth of who you are by needing to *become* that person in order to experience success, how ever you may define it.

During my journey of spiritual liberation, I encountered the part of me that was very driven by the need to achieve. Even in the midst of my spiritual paralysis, I was a really "good achiever." I achieved many things: recovering from compulsive eating, bulimia and a weight problem; getting a business degree; trading stocks and bonds with the "big boys" while making great money and becoming an assistant vice president by the age of twenty-four; going back to school later in life to get a masters degree in social work by the age of thirty-four; completely changing careers to create my own private practice; meeting, falling in love with, and marrying my soul-mate; overcoming fertility challenges to have two healthy, beautiful children; buying and living on our dream vineyard; becoming wine-makers and sellers; traveling all over the world, healing family relationships ... and the journey continues.

I tell you this not to boast but to share the most surprising discovery I made along the way. Like many people, I wanted a lot. I thought that if I filled these wants, I'd be happy. However, as I started to reach my goals, I learned that happiness did not come from their achievement. Instead happiness came through discovering who I needed to *become* in order to realize these goals.

What happened was that, as I achieved some goals, I discovered they did not represent who I was or wanted to be in my life. Consequently, my goals and dreams evolved as I allowed the truth of who I was on the inside to shine and be expressed on the outside. I began to see my true self expressing through my relationships, through my work, and through every commitment I made. I've come to a place now where every aspect of my life is an honest expression of who I am and what I believe in. *That* is success for the soul. And that is the opportunity available through this book. Now, here's a question for you:

Which areas of your life are HONEST expressions of who you really are?

Take a moment to really ponder this question. Listen for your answer before you read on ...

If you answered:
- Anything less than "ALL the areas of my life," or
- "I don't know who I really am," or
- "I don't understand the question,"

then this book most likely has something to offer you. If you answered: "Every aspect of my life is an honest expression of who I really am," then know that if you are compelled to read on, it's probably because there's something here that can help you to become even *more* of who you are.

So, what I'm offering you are all the tools I know *work* to make your dreams come true and an opportunity to discover and express who you really are in the process of making those dreams come true. I'm sure you will find discovering and expressing who you really are is much more fulfilling than any dream you could ever realize. Those dreams are indeed realized, but they become a by-product of the dream you may not have even known you had:

**Be yourself, your soul's truth,
fully expressed in all areas of your life.**

Enjoy the ride!

2

How to Use This Book

People read self-help books to help themselves, right? Right. But there's a problem with books. They only engage your cerebral self. It takes more than pondering a few good ideas to change your life. Ninety percent of what it takes to manifest success for the soul is *not* intellectual in nature; it is spiritual, emotional and physical. So, just like anything in life, you will get out of it what you put into it. If you simply read the book, your synapses will fire for a while but your life will remain unchanged. If, however, you take the opportunity to give yourself to the exercises, questions and opportunities for reflection, you will be taking full advantage of this book's offering.

In your hands you hold a catalyst for a transformational approach to personal success. That being said, I'd like to offer you two ways you might approach this material. One way is to read the entire book from beginning to end, marking the exercises you'd like to return to later. This will give you the opportunity to first get an overview of the concepts. Then, when you return to the exercises, you'll have a broader context for the insights they might offer you. The other approach is to do the exercises that speak to you as you go. If you do so, you may experience this book as an unfolding journey right from the beginning. The advantage to this is that each insight you glean from the exercises will build upon the next as The Mystic's Formula reveals itself to you. If you go with this second method, decide right now that you will trust the process. You may not always know where you're headed, but you will complete the book having traveled a personal journey of opening and awakening.

As with all things, there is no right way to do this. There is only **your** way. Trust what feels good to you. If you try an exercise and it just doesn't click, move on. Don't let yourself get stuck if something isn't gelling for you. You can always come back to it later with fresh eyes and a new perspective. The main thing is to keep moving forward.

A Little Disclaimer

There is another thing about which I want to be perfectly clear: My objective through this book is to convey to you practical and completely "doable" methods for making your dreams come true. A lot of what I cover in this book could be explained in very esoteric, scientific, complicated, and intellectual ways. Someone might read this and say, "Well, that's not entirely accurate." This book is not meant to be a scholarly endeavor for scientific research ... theorizing, hypothesizing, and proving. This book is for you to use! And so, for those who are not new to the realm of personal success, you may perceive some of these concepts to be presented in simple ways. However, just because something is simple does not mean it isn't powerful. I've discovered there are many people who have been into personal growth and actualization for years who still find themselves blocked or stuck. For you, I say, read on! Profound truth is oftentimes incredibly simple, and sometimes it is the simplified presentation of something that helps you break through those very blocks that keep you stuck.

3

The "G" Word

"You might as well not be alive if you're not in awe of God."

— *Albert Einstein (1879-1955)*
physicist, Nobel Prize winner

The "G" word refers to the word *God*. Yes, I will be talking about God in this book – in different ways and with different words. The truth is, you can't pursue success for the soul without talking about God. And, because this small, three-letter word can represent a highly charged subject for many people, it is important for you, the reader, to feel clear about and comfortable with the meaning that will be associated with the word God in the context of this book's message.

God means many things to many people. For some, the word and concept of God is very comforting. For others, it is quite uncomfortable and/or conflicting, complete with challenging emotions such as fear, guilt, anger or confusion. And yet for others, it is uncharted territory.

We will go into this with more detail soon enough but for right now, know that within the context of this book, God is defined as an infinite intelligence that is the source of all that is. Throughout the book, I'll use terms like Infinite Intelligence, Source, Divine Spirit, The One, Consciousness and Energy. These terms will be used interchangeably. This infinite intelligence is the one power, the one presence, and the one life that manifests in, as, and through you, me and all the universe. It is the beginning and the end. It is eternal. He/She/It is all-loving, all-powerful, all-knowing and all-good. There is no talk of the devil, sin or evil. None of that. God is love. God is harmony. God is perfect health and infinite well-being. God is abundance and prosperity. God is peace. God is good.

As for the word *soul*, this refers to a deeper, broader aspect of you that has access to Infinite Intelligence. Since we assume here that there is one and only one energy, it follows that you *must be* a part of that same energy. You are an individualized expression of Divine Spirit. As a result, you embody, experience and express the very same qualities. You are made up of the same substance. And the only thing that has you experience yourself and your life as less than infinite and limitless is your consciousness – that aspect of your *human* consciousness that limits your perception through thoughts and belief systems. In this book, I use different terms interchangeably for the word *soul* – words like Higher Self, Inner Being, and Inner Knowing.

This book is about spirituality, not religion. You will not be asked to adopt or sacrifice any particular set of beliefs. You will simply be offered a way of looking at how the universe works based on universal laws. If something does not ring true for you, put it aside for the time being. It might have different meaning for you in the future. Or, see if you can reinterpret the idea in a way or a language that is more to your liking. Success for the soul is about discovering *your* truth, *your* heart's desire, the source of *your* fulfillment and peace.

4

The Mystic's Formula™

mys·ti·cism (mis'ta siz'em) *n.* the doctrine of an immediate
spiritual intuition of truths believed to transcend ordinary
understanding, or of a direct, intimate union of the soul with God
through contemplation or spiritual ecstasy...

— *Webster's Dictionary*

In order to experience success for the soul, you must travel a
mystical journey. It is important to understand that mysticism
isn't as mysterious as it may sound. Mysticism is simply a matter of broadening your perspective. Mysticism is about opening
up to a way of perceiving life beyond your five senses. It is about
waking up to the fact that you are much larger than the you
that you see in the mirror. As you open up and wake up to an
expanded definition of self, you begin to tap into the power you
already have to create the life of your dreams.

So, how do you create success for the soul? Where, exactly,
does one begin on this journey of making dreams come true?
Wouldn't a formula be nice? Well, I have a formula. Once I share
it, you may think, "Oh brother! How trite is *that?*" Or, you may
want to toss this book out the window. Or you may be relieved to
know you're on the right path. Or you may think, "I've heard
this before and it hasn't worked. What's going to be different
this time?"

I call this The Mystic's Formula because it is based in a timeless wisdom that transcends ordinary understanding. The formula I'm about to share has been practiced, studied, dissected, revered and misinterpreted through the ages. It has been translated and expounded by philosophers, clerics, physicists, motivational speakers, spiritualists and poets. It is based on Universal Cosmic Law and it works – *if* you know how to interpret and use it correctly. This formula is nothing less than the secret of life. That's right. You heard me. *The secret of life!* And once you begin to truly understand, and more importantly *see* how it works in your life, you'll scratch your head wondering how we got so off track.

Are you ready? Here it is. The formula for making any and all of your dreams come true is:

Step I. **Identify what you want.**
Step II. **Pretend you already have it.**
Step III. **Step out of your own way.**
Step IV. **Welcome it into your life.**

That's it. Very simple, yes? Yes. But simple doesn't mean easy. And the rest of this book is all about understanding how to interpret and use this formula *correctly* and how to navigate your way through the inevitable bumps you will hit along the way.

Integrating this formula into your way of seeing the universe and integrating it in your life is a process of expanding your consciousness. Expanding your consciousness is a growing process. And growing is hard sometimes, hence the term *growing pains*. It is these growing pains that, when misunderstood as irreparable failure or fatal flaws, has us quit on our dreams and/or this formula. Do yourself a favor. Don't quit before the miracle ... because miracles are yours to be had!

Through the ages, wise ones have understood that we each possess the power to create our own reality. They've understood exactly how this is done, and they have sought to be messengers of this knowledge. For these wise ones have known that when you know this truth and understand it, you will be set free.

PROPHETS

"We are what we think. All that we are arises with our thoughts.
With our thoughts we make our world."

— *The Buddha*

PSYCHOLOGISTS

"The greatest discovery of my generation is that a human being
can alter his life by altering his attitude of mind."

— *William James (1842-1910)*
U.S. psychologist and philosopher

SCIENTISTS

"Considered together, Bohm and Pribram's theories provide a
profound new way of looking at the world: Our brains
mathematically construct objective reality by interpreting
frequencies that are ultimately projections from another
dimension, a deeper order of existence that is beyond both space
and time: The brain is a hologram enfolded in a holographic
universe."

— *Michael Talbot*
author, The Holographic Universe *on theories of David Bohm,*
quantum physicist, and Karl Pribram, neurophysiologist

POLITICIANS

"Dream lofty dreams, and as you dream, so you shall become.
Your vision is the promise of what you shall one day be; your ideal
is the prophecy of what you shall at last unveil."

— *James Allen (1855-1942)*
New Zealander statesman, Minister of Defense

SPIRITUAL MEDIUMS

"Intend it, and allow it, and it is."

— *Esther Hicks*
teachings of Abraham

PHILOSOPHERS

"The universe is transformation; our life is what our thoughts
make it."

— *Marcus Aurelius (121-180)*
philosopher, emperor of Rome

METAPHYSICIANS

"Our thought is operated on by a universal creativity which is infinite in its capacity to accomplish. Thus, in taking thought we do not force anything, we merely decide what thought to follow, knowing that the result is automatic."

— Ernest Holmes (1887-1960)
founder, Science of Mind

ARTISTS

"Everything you can imagine is real."

— Pablo Picasso (1882-1972)
Spanish artist and painter

POETS

"If one advances confidently in the direction of his dream, and endeavors to live the life which he has imagined, he will meet with a success unexpected in common hours."

— Henry David Thoreau (1817-1862)
American author, transcendentalist, philosopher

5

How The Formula Works

Metaphysics 101

Before we delve more deeply into The Mystic's Formula, we are going to spend some time exploring why and how it works. The underlying principles that are expressed throughout the use of The Formula are metaphysical. Rooted in the Greek language, *meta* means *after* or *beyond* and *physics* pertains to *nature,* or *the physical* (i.e., that which you can perceive through your five physical senses). Hence, when I refer to metaphysics, I mean *beyond the physical.* The inner workings of The Formula are beyond the physical, beyond the obvious. The Formula works because it harnesses and directs energy – something that is very real but cannot be seen. We will be looking at the source of things rather than the effect. We will be looking at problems rather than symptoms, at solutions rather than fixes.

There is much to learn in the world of metaphysics from the practical to the mystical, from the scientific to the mysterious. For our purposes, we are going to focus on a few fundamental principles as they apply to manifesting the life of your dreams. The principles are very simple but applying and integrating them into your consciousness and life can be a different story. Some people learn a few tools and are content to improve their lives a little. Other people put themselves on a lifelong path, ever-expanding upon their experience of freedom, joy, growth, abundance, success and fulfillment. The tools and concepts of metaphysics deal with the unalterable laws of the universe. We are subjected to and affected by these laws every moment of our lives. To the degree we understand these concepts, we are able to become masters of our lives. To the degree we are unaware of these concepts, we may perceive ourselves to be at the mercy of circumstance or fate.

Fundamental Principles

There is Only ONE

- There is only one source for ALL that exists in the universe. **Since there is only ONE – the only, the every, the all of All That Is – then YOU, like everything else, are made up of this Source Energy.**

- Hence you are the embodiment of this Source Energy and possess within you all of the properties and expressions of this energy.

The ONE is Love

- This Source Energy is, by nature, omnipotent (all powerful), omnipresent (everywhere), omniscient (all knowing), omni-beneficent (all good).

  Consequently this energy is:
  - **Divine love, perfect health, limitless wealth and success, fulfillment in every way.**
  - **Infinite (absolutely without limitation of any kind).**
  - **Impersonal, non-judgmental, neutral.**
  - **Unconditional (under all circumstances and conditions).**

Like Attracts Like

- Whatever you offer the Universe in thought and emotion, you attract back into your life as a physical equivalent.

Proof or Faith?

The above fundamental principles are the basic assumptions upon which The Mystic's Formula is constructed. If these assumptions are already aligned with your belief systems, it will be easy for you to proceed with learning and practicing The Formula.

If, however, you just can't buy into these assumptions (perhaps they scare you, you may feel they are in direct conflict with your religious beliefs or your concept of reality, you might believe only in what you can see or touch, or you simply need proof), then I have a few things for you to ponder before you proceed.

There was a time, not too long ago, that the fundamental principles could only have been taken on faith or personal experience. If neither of these was accessible to you, you'd have been among those unlucky enough to miss out on an opportunity to tap into the great mystery of life.

Fortunately, we live in a time where our technology is now able to demonstrate some of these principles. Regarding the first principle, *There is only ONE*, I will offer you a beautiful summary of scientific findings as presented by Lynne McTaggart in the prologue of her book, *The Field: The Quest for the Secret Force of the Universe*:

"For a number of decades respected scientists in a variety of disciplines all over the world have been carrying out well-designed experiments whose results fly in the face of current biology and physics. Together these studies offer us copious information about the central organizing force governing our bodies and the rest of the cosmos.

What they have discovered is nothing less than astonishing. At our most elemental, we are not a chemical reaction, but an energetic charge. Human beings and all living things are a coalescence of energy in a field of energy connected to every other thing in the world. This pulsating energy field is the central engine of our being and our consciousness, the alpha and the omega of our existence.

There is no 'me' and 'not-me' duality to our bodies in relation to the universe, but one underlying energy field. This field is responsible for our mind's highest functions, the information source guiding the growth of our bodies. It is our brain, our heart, our memory – indeed, a blueprint of the world for all time. The field is the force, rather than germs or genes, that finally determines whether we are healthy or ill, the force which must be tapped in order to heal. We are attached and engaged, indivisible from our world, and our only fundamental truth is our relationship with it. 'The field,' as Einstein once succinctly put it, 'is the only reality.'"

Science also supports the second principle: *Like Attracts Like*. It has been demonstrated that, at the subatomic level, reality is malleable to the consciousness of the observer. Quantum physics specifically teaches us that reality isn't what we thought it was. We used to think of reality as a physical, concrete dimension outside of ourselves. However, quantum physics is showing us that what we used to think of as tangible matter actually changes form – from particle to wave – depending on whether or not we are looking at it. In wave form, when we're not looking, there is only possibility. However, when we observe something, the wave collapses into a particle. Our consciousness, our choices and our expectations impact the form of reality.

One remarkable demonstration of this can be seen in the work of Dr. Masaru Emoto. In his book, *The Hidden Messages in Water*, Dr. Emoto describes his research of the effects of human thought and emotion on water. With high-speed photography, he has captured the crystal formations produced by water exposed to a wide variety of visual imagery, music, and written words. Thoughts and emotions, more joyful, loving and positive in nature, produced symmetrical, bright, snowflake-like crystals. The more fearful, angry or negative thoughts and emotions produced irregular, duller and darker formations.

As for the fundamental principle, *The ONE is Love*, we are harder-pressed to find scientific support here. There is plenty of debate over whether the Universe is finite or infinite. But, how does one measure love, at least scientifically speaking? At this juncture, we must leap to the realm of faith, or at very least, willingness.

If you are to learn and practice The Mystic's Formula with any success, you must, at the very least, be *willing* to consider that the fundamental principles are true. If you are not at least willing, it simply won't work.

This is because inherent in The Mystic's Formula is a "Catch-22." The underlying assumption is that your consciousness creates your reality. But your consciousness must *believe* that your consciousness creates your reality. If your consciousness believes that you *don't* create your reality, then your consciousness will create *that* experience.

If you are convinced that we live in a horrible world of suffering, that God is judgmental and punishing, or that you are a victim in a random, chaotic Universe, this principle will be a big, tough pill to swallow. You may be completely justified in your suffering. However, if you feel stuck and unable to conceive of the possibility of a benevolent Universe, could you at least consider the possibility that you're wrong? Haven't you been wrong at least once or twice in your life? And if you were wrong then, isn't it possible you're wrong now?

The Leap of Faith

"For what is faith unless it is to believe what you do not see?"
— *St. Augustine (354-430)*
Roman Catholic saint

The question to ask yourself is, "Would I rather continue to believe I am right, or would I rather be happy?" If you'd rather be happy, you are going to have to be *willing* to be happy, which means you will have to let go of the belief that your reality just happens to you. You will have to be willing to believe you have control over your experience.

Even if you cannot fully embrace the fundamental principles, you *can* successfully proceed with The Mystic's Formula if you are open and willing to suspend judgment. So, if you want to give this a good, honest try – if you realize that what you've been doing up until now hasn't worked – then do this: While you're reading this book, or for the next 40 days (whichever is greater), anytime doubt or judgment comes into your mind, repeat this mantra with sincere intention:

**"I am WILLING to discover and experience
the highest possibility of good in my life."**

If you do only this, you will experience positive changes in your life. Try it! You have nothing to lose but 40 days of being right about your misery and the cost of this book.

Using the Principles in Your Life

So now that you know the fundamental principles and are in the right frame of mind for learning, let's talk about how it is that you create your reality. Here's what happens when you manifest something in your life:

You have a thought, an idea, which you think about. That thought may or may not trigger an emotional response within you. All emotion magnetizes, so to speak, that thought, drawing unto it similar thoughts (remember like attracts like). The more you think about that thought with emotion, the more powerful the magnetic quality is of that idea, or energy formation, until ultimately, you draw into your experience that idea in physical form.

The emotional energy flowing through you and flowing through this thought determines two major conditions regarding how you experience your manifestation. These conditions are:

1. The speed with which this thought manifests into your experience, and
2. Whether or not the thought manifests in a positive way (aligned with your desires) or a negative way (contrary to your desires).

It follows then that if you could learn how to truly harness this powerful emotional energy, you would express tremendous power in manifesting what you desire.

This process of manifestation is 100% guaranteed, always, without condition. It is law. It is the Law of Attraction.

But, But, But ...

I know, I know, I've thought it. Ninety-nine percent of the earthly population thinks it. How could that possibly be true? There are things in my life I've been thinking about forever that, to this day, have never come true. I have things that come into my life that I rarely, if ever think about, and do not want. The answer lies in the *kinds* of thoughts you entertain about a desire and the subsequent *emotions* you perpetuate. It is through understanding these all important subtleties that you can become a master of the art and science of manifestation.

You Are a Sending and Receiving Station

Everything is energy – everything you see and everything you don't see. You are energy. The book in your hands is energy. Your body is energy. Your thoughts are energy. Your emotions are energy. In other words, everything is vibrating. And that which determines the unique qualities of any given thing – the aspects and qualities that make an apple an apple instead of an orange – is wavelength and frequency. This energy of All That Is is infinite. The essential substance of everything that has ever been or will ever be already exists as pure energy. Every thought that has ever been thought exists as an energy formation. So, everything you could ever want essentially already exists – as energy.

Then, if what I want already exists as energy, how do I bring what I want into my experience? Remember the fundamental principle – *like attracts like*. The way you bring what you desire into your life is to match its vibration. And you match its vibration through your thoughts and emotions. In other words, you could think of yourself as a living, breathing magnet, or a sending and receiving station. The vibration you radiate or emit through your thoughts and emotions is the vibration you magnetically draw into your life in the form of its manifested equivalent.

For example, when your attention is on money, the experience you draw into your life will depend on the thoughts and feelings you resonate with, or the vibration you emit regarding money. Although words are powerful, it is the emotional energy and the belief systems underneath that determine their magnetic quality. If you think or say, "I want money," you will attract into your experience *you wanting money*. Although you could think about, dream about, fantasize about and talk about having lots of money, if your underlying feelings and beliefs are, "I never have enough money," you manifest in your experience *you never having enough money*.

It is possible to articulate the same words *I want money* and be a very prosperous person because the underlying feelings and beliefs are those of *havingness, abundance* and *prosperity*. I can guarantee you that if Donald Trump said, "I want money!" ten million dollars would appear *poof* in a pile on the table in front of him. If a poor person declared those same words, chances are pretty good the table would remain bare. Yes, I'm kidding around a bit here, but the point I'm trying to make is that it's not the words themselves that are magnetic, but the underlying consciousness. Donald Trump's existing prosperity consciousness (the thoughts and feelings of, "I have lots of money") is what would draw to him the experience of *having lots of money* – his next ten million as a matter of fact. It is the scarcity consciousness (the thoughts and feelings of *there is never enough, we're broke*) of the poor person that draws to him *not having enough* and *being broke*.

So there you have it, the first lesson of metaphysics. These energetic laws create your reality every day of your life. As you direct your thoughts and emotions, consciously or not, you set in motion the Law of Attraction. And thought by thought, emotion upon emotion, you choose among infinite possibilities the life experience that will unfold before you. The more you understand and practice The Mystic's Formula, the more you will develop the skills necessary to direct these energies exactly as you would choose. Now then, onto Step I of The Formula!

THE MYSTIC'S FORMULA
Step I:

Identify What You Want

6

Your Wanting Mechanism

"There is a space between man's imagination and man's attainment that may only be traversed by his longing."

— Kahlil Gibran (1883-1931)
essayist, novelist, poet

In my earlier days as a workshop facilitator, I used to say, "There are two small words that distinguish successful people – those who have the lives they desire – from unsuccessful people – those who do not have the lives they desire. Those two words are *I want.*"

You have inside you a wanting mechanism. When you want something, every part of your being responds. How your being responds, however, depends on how you relate to your wanting. There are empowering ways to relate to your wanting and disempowering ways. There is wanting from your soul and wanting from your ego, which we will explore at length in future chapters. In this chapter, we will explore all the facets of wanting and discovering the power of this creative spark in your life.

Activating your internal wanting mechanism is the first and very important step in The Mystic's Formula. One way to look at this whole manifestation machine is to view your wanting mechanism as the ignition, the Law of Attraction as the engine (it does all of the work), and your thoughts and emotions aligned with Source Energy as the fuel (the energy that brings it to life). A number of levels of awareness operate when you use your wanting mechanism. One level is *knowing* what you want.

Another level is *letting yourself want* what you want. And yet another level is *focusing* on what you want, as opposed to focusing on what you *don't* want. In this chapter, you will be learning more about activating your wanting mechanism through working with these different levels of awareness. The more aware you become, and the more you practice directing your awareness, the easier it will be for you to effectively utilize step one of The Formula.

There are a number of ways to identify what you want. Some methods are simple; some are more involved. In this chapter, we'll be reviewing five methods for identifying what you want:

1. Noticing the Dissonance
2. The Detective Method
3. The Brainstorming Method
4. The Collage Method, and
5. The Vision Workshop.

All of these methods will help you exercise your awareness muscle. In other words, all of these methods will help you to *know* what you want, *allow yourself to want* what you want, and *focus* on what you want.

Obstacles to Identifying What You Want

However ... before we start exploring the different methods for identifying what you want, it is important to acknowledge that many people struggle with obstacles that can stop them before they even get started. Better to deal with these inner demons from the very beginning because they have a nasty way of bursting our bubbles.

The two greatest obstacles to identifying what you want are **fear** – the fear of letting yourself want what you want, and **bad habit** – the habit of having most of your attention focused on what you do *not* want.

The Fear Obstacle

When you begin to explore your wants, you may find yourself hearing the voices of fear. These voices ...

- Make you think you don't know what you want, or that you don't want anything.
- Make you feel doubt.
- Sound like limiting beliefs passed on to you by parents, teachers, friends, society, TV, etc.
- Sound like, *"Yeah, but... Yeah, but... Yeah, but..."*

These are all smoke screens that distract you from letting your wanting mechanism do its job, which is to activate the creative spark that sets the manifesting machine in motion.

The truth is that you know exactly what you want – at least somewhere deep down inside – even if it isn't easily accessible. We all want. Wanting is the most natural, God-given characteristic we embody. If you don't let it flow and express itself to and through you, you might as well be dead. As a matter of fact, if you are one of those people who has stifled, suppressed, repressed or choked down your wants, you may feel dead. If this is the case, be gentle with yourself. Having your wanting mechanism shut down is often the result of painful experiences or messages you received in your past, sometimes from parents, sometimes from school, from "friends," well-meaning strangers or the media. The truth is, there are plenty of places we can find naysayers along the way to burst our bubbles or discourage us. But guess what? There are plenty of supportive, encouraging, uplifting, inspiring cheerleaders, friends, role models, strangers, coaches, teachers, etc., too. It all depends on whether or not you will *let* yourself want what you want.

The Bad Habit Obstacle

"Argue for your limitations, and sure enough, they're yours."
— *Richard Bach (1936-)*
American writer

When you fall into *bad habit* (which can and does happen to the best of us, and sometimes often), you tend to do more than your fair share of complaining, criticizing, doubting and identifying the inadequacies or shortcomings of other people or situations. You might hear or see positive people and want to vomit, or not trust them, or see them as sickeningly Pollyanna or *too happy* (whatever *that* means!) You may feel irritable or negative or discontent. And the interesting thing about this is that, many times, the only reason you're in this yucky place is because you've fallen prey to the bad habit of putting your attention on that which you *do not want*. I'm not saying that you may not have some genuine reason for discontent. But, **happiness has everything to do with choosing how you focus your attention.** Expressions like, *Life is 90% attitude and 10% what happens to you,* and *Some people see the glass as half empty and some see it as half full* reflect this age-old wisdom.

The bad habit of focusing on the negative is seductive and powerful because it is familiar and there is no shortage of support (i.e., people around us all too eager to hop on the negativity bandwagon). However, as long as you keep focusing on what you do *not* want, all you will get is more of what you do not want. If you change your habit and begin looking at what you *do* want, you will begin seeing and experiencing more of what you do want. (Have you ever noticed how, when you discover a favorite new car, you start seeing it everywhere?)

If you have fallen victim to the addiction of negative thinking, nothing less than sheer discipline, and a lot of faith, can change the course of your experience – at least in the beginning.

But, once you've built up enough momentum to see the positive in your life begin to expand – and this takes 30 to 40 days – discipline will be replaced by the fulfillment of focusing on what you want and experiencing more of that in your life.

Okay, so hopefully you've gotten the message. You've got to let yourself want what you want before you can know what you want. And you've got to be willing to focus on what you want, *not* what you *don't* want, if you're going to let into your experience what you want.

When You Don't Know What You Want

The Universe has set things up for us here on planet Earth to make the task of knowing what we want quite easy actually. We live in the realm of duality. We live in a world where everything is relative to everything else. Abraham-Hicks, who teaches *The*

Art of Allowing, calls it *living in contrast.* And it is in this realm of contrast that you get to notice the difference between what you want and what you have.

At the risk of going off on a tangent right about now, I'd like to answer an age-old question that goes something like, "How can God exist if there is so much pain and suffering in the world?" Why am I interjecting this philosophical question here and now? Because the answer to this question is pivotal to manifesting your dreams and identifying what you want.

There is pain and suffering in the world because the greatest gift of being human is to be surrounded by the contrast of what you like and what you don't like, so you can decide what you want. If there were no contrast, no relativity, there would be no environment from which to birth new desire. Can you imagine what your life would be like if you had no desire? We'd all be walking zombies. Sure, maybe there would be no war because there would be no desires to fight over. But there would be no joy, for there would be no desire to compel us toward anything that moves us or makes us feel alive!

The ironic twist is that you know there is a God *because* there is pain and suffering. Are you scratching your head now, asking, "HUH?" Well, this is how it works: First and foremost we are eternal beings. Our souls are eternal. And we move around through different experiences such as being in physical form and being in nonphysical form. In the nonphysical, we re-emerge into the realm of the absolute or God-consciousness, where we know and "remember" divine love. However, besides being eternal, we are creative. Better yet, we are creators! We desire to experience and create and expand ever more. So, we created the experience we recognize as the physical realm. In the absolute, we are one with the absolute so we *know* love, *know* joy, *know* freedom, etc. In other words, our consciousness is one with the realm of All That Is. In the physical realm, we get to experience and create from what we know. So, we have access to All That Is and all that is not, too. Therefore, in the physical realm:

- There is love AND the absence of love (such as fear, hate, envy ...).
- There is joy AND the absence of joy (discontent, anger, doubt ...).

- There is abundance AND the absence of abundance (poverty, scarcity, need ...).
- There is perfect health AND the absence of perfect health (illness, suffering, pain ...).

And from this relativity or contrast, we experience preferences. We experience desires. With this spark of desire, we activate our creative power and the process of manifestation. It is this creative process that will unfold and become clearer as you read on. So, back to the age-old question: **there *is* a God, and God is within YOU as co-creator of your experience. *We*, as a part of the ONE Source, created the realm of contrast (love, joy, freedom AND pain, suffering, hate) so as to provide the catalyst for desire, which allows us to experience and express ourselves as creators. (I promise this *will* make more sense as you go on.)**

What does this all have to do with wanting? Everything. Wanting is your soul being YOU fully expressed. Wanting is God's gift to you. Wanting is God expressing through you. Wanting is the first step in creating what you want. If you don't let yourself want, you will never have. As a result of all this, wanting will lead you home to your true Self, because as you want, you discover more of what you want and what you don't want. And this, in turn, allows you to discover more and more of who you are and who you are not, IF (and this is a BIG if) you follow the wanting with the rest of the formula, which includes *allowing* yourself to *have* what you want.

This is what success for the soul is all about. It is in daring to want that you dare to let your soul shine. Because there is no way to have what you want without being YOU fully expressed. Oh sure, you can pull what you want into your life through an internal place of lack, but through that venue, what you want won't stay very long and it certainly won't make you happy. For example, did you ever hear about people who win the lottery and within a short time lose everything and their lives are ruined? The only thing that will make you happy is to be YOU fully expressed, i.e., letting your soul shine through, feeling full vs. lacking, feeling whole vs. full of holes. When you do that, YOU are fulfilled (full-filled) and guess what? Your dreams are magnetically drawn into your life because like attracts like! You ARE joy, abundance and having. So, you draw to yourself more joy, abundance and having. It doesn't get much better than that!

"The mark of your ignorance is the depth of your belief in injustice and tragedy. What the caterpillar calls the end of the world, the master calls a butterfly."

— *Richard Bach*

7

How to Identify What You Want

"Every person is unique. Shakespeare will never be made by the
study of Shakespeare. Do that which is assigned to you, and you
cannot [dream too large] or dare too much."

— *Ralph Waldo Emerson (1803-1882)*
American author, poet, philosopher

What follows are five techniques that will help you not only
identify what you want, but begin attracting it into your
life. You can mix and match these exercises any way you want,
or pick just one that is *your thing*. It is not uncommon for men
to gravitate towards different techniques than women. All the
techniques are fun and powerful in different ways. Personally,
I use all of these techniques, playing around with the one that
inspires me the most at any given moment. In my current state
of evolution, my wanting mechanism looks like me living my
life:

- Trying to notice the contrast when I'm finding myself
  reacting to something or someone I dislike, and making
  a mental note of what I would prefer instead.
- Practicing putting my attention on what makes me feel
  good.
- Attempting always to be in gratitude, usually making a
  big life brainstorming list at the beginning of each new
  year, and little manifest lists on my dry-erase board in
  the kitchen when I have a list of wants that keep bugging me, but I have no idea how I will manifest.

Sometimes I get infused with a dose of inspiration and create a collage or write a vision which I frame and email to my friends. And whenever I see people who have qualities, things or lives I want, rather than feel jealousy, resentment or judgment, I *always* see it as an opportunity to expand my consciousness, becoming a detective and identifying more of what I want in my experience.

Technique #1 – Noticing Dissonance

The first technique we will explore is *Noticing Dissonance.* When you use this technique, you will begin identifying what you want by noticing when you are experiencing something you do *not* want. Dissonance is defined as: "lack of harmony, lack of resolution, incongruence."

When you notice dissonance, you are noticing the lack of harmony or disagreement between that which you want and that which you currently have. Many times we perpetuate what we don't want because something we don't want happens in our lives, so we react to it, give it lots of attention and emotional energy, and magnetically draw more of what we don't want to us. It is in making conscious our unconscious reaction that we have the power to activate our wanting mechanism. The trick to this method is to STOP *in the moment* of our reaction to what we don't want and say to ourselves,

> **"Ahhh! This is dissonance. I *don't* want this.
> What would I *want* instead?"**

This technique is very simple. *The most difficult part about it is waking up in the middle of your reaction!* If you can do this (and it does get easier with practice), this technique is an incredibly potent catalyst for changing what you experience in your life.

Exercise

Think about something that has been an ongoing struggle or challenge in your life, something that has consistently gotten lots of your mental and emotional energy. As you take into account the metaphysical principles we reviewed in Chapter 5 and how the Law of Attraction works, think about just how much powerful energy you've been putting into that problem. A lot, right? You think about it, you fume over it, you worry, you talk about it, you have emotions over it. That's a lot of magnetic energy you're infusing into that topic in your life. The result? All that you do *not* want is getting lots and lots of energy.

The next time that *thing* happens and you begin to react to it, mentally STOP and think, "Ahhh! This is dissonance. I *don't want* this. What would I *want* instead?" And then redirect all of your mental and emotional energy towards what you want? Really go for it. Think about what you want. Talk to yourself about it. Write about it. It doesn't matter when or where, just start putting energy into what you want – either in the moment or later. Do whatever you can do to put your attention on something that makes you feel good as opposed to feeling bad. What do you want? Why do you want it? How does it make you feel to imagine yourself having what you want? Feel it. See it. Put all the emotion and sensory feeling you can muster into it. The more you do this, the more you will begin attracting what you want rather than what you do not want.

Guiding Your Inner Toddler

This technique has the potential to evolve into a mental way of life. At first, your greatest accomplishment will be to notice where your mind goes and choosing a different direction. It will take effort and discipline. Eventually, you can evolve to a place where you gently and regularly catch your thoughts before they get you into trouble – like a loving parent who consistently redirects their one-year-old child away from unsafe situations to safe situations. The parent doesn't think about it. The act of loving redirection is a natural instinct.

One of my common personal pitfalls for dissonance used to occur with people I'd find incompetent or irritating. When I first started noticing dissonance, I usually wouldn't notice it until I'd worked myself up to quite a self-righteous lather of discontent. "Uggh, that guy is so slow! Can't people just do their job. Helloooo! Isn't it obvious that there are ten people waiting in line? Could you have your little chat over a cup of coffee on someone else's time! Grrr." By the time I'd realize I was experiencing dissonance, I'd have spent a good chunk of time sighing and rolling my eyes, while I energized with all of my attention the very thing I *didn't* want. Once I woke up, I'd eventually yell in my head, "Oh dissonance! Right! I don't want this. Instead I want EASE AND GRACE. Okay, deeeep breath. I intend ease and grace in all that I do under all conditions! I see myself dealing with the nicest, most competent people I've ever met. I'm open and receptive to good unfolding for me every second of my day!"

Eventually, my mind developed the loving, watchful parent over my complaining toddler-mind. So, now, I barely sigh at the slow clerk and hear in my mind, "Oh yeah, ease and grace." Or, I'm running late and getting stressed. My mind begins, "Grrr ... stinking traffic ... oh yeah, ease and grace. Time expands. No worries." It really can become quite effortless.

By noticing dissonance as a way of life, you identify what you want, moment by moment. By the Law of Attraction, one thought builds on the next thought and in 30 to 40 days, you'll build up so much momentum that ease and grace become your new default, more and more of the time.

Technique #2 – The Detective Method

The Detective Method is a very fun and effective method for identifying what you want. All it requires is for you to open your eyes and ears to the world around you and make mental notes of what you like and what you'd want in your life. You are essentially creating a composite image or role model by gathering together bits and pieces from the people, things and situations you observe. I've often recommended this technique to clients who seek to create the relationship of their dreams. As much as they know they want a relationship, and they want to be in love and feeling good, and they don't want to get hurt, when I ask them for a clearer sense of the qualities and dynamics of their dream relationship, they struggle to find the words. Many clients don't even know if what they want is possible. Or they discover that the relationships that have captured their attention are either based in the fantasy of television and movies or the fallout of failed marriages. Maybe their parents had a relationship they do not want to emulate, but they can't imagine one that would feel satisfying.

With this method, you are giving yourself the assignment of acting like a detective. Every day, you are to wake up and set your intention to find examples of things you like and want in your life. If you know you want to create the relationship of your dreams, start by looking at the relationships that exist in your own world among family, friends, colleagues and strangers. Listen, look and sense. "Hey, I like the way each seems to know what the other needs without saying much. I like the way they seem to be able to compromise with such grace. I love how much fun they always seem to have together. I like that they have so much in common. I like that they are so different, yet somehow they are a perfect complement to each other." As you identify what you like, make a mental note – or even better a written note – and watch your composite role-model take shape as you continue to gather information.

If you dream of financial freedom, get specific and start gathering information. "I love how he never seems to worry about money. I love how generous she is. I like that his wealth came from something he created from the ground up. I love that her wealth came from doing something she loves. I love that he has so much money and even though people seem to judge him unfairly, he still seems so genuine and down to earth. I love how comfortable she seems to be with her wealth. I love that he succeeded despite his past failures."

If your dream is to transform your physical body towards greater health, well-being and beauty look around and find your role models. There are many roads to the same destination, not all will be the right or fulfilling road for you. "I like that she is more committed to her health than meeting some unrealistic standard. I like that he has integrated exercise into his life in such a consistent yet workable way. I like that she seems to love herself wherever she is on her journey to losing weight. I really like the way he fits exercise into his life by doing competitive sports instead of the boring old gym. I like that she did the mental and emotional work to make the necessary life-style changes instead of just obsessing over the next fad-diet. I love seeing the way she found a way to make herself a priority instead of always putting herself last on the list."

Remember, you can do this easily for any and every part of your life – any dream you may hold for yourself. When you use this method, not only will you begin to have greater clarity about what you want, but by simply starting to put your attention on it with enthusiasm, you will attract to yourself more of what you want. The key is to have fun with this. If you're going to use this method, do so in the spirit of fun, of discovering the endless possibilities. And always remember, if it is possible in the world, it is possible for you. This is because there is only one Source and the same substance that made it possible for others lives in, as, and through you, too.

Technique #3 – The Brainstorming Method

If you choose to experiment with the Brainstorming Method, you'll need a notebook and pen (or computer) and quiet, uninterrupted time. The first time out with the exercise, it is good to give yourself a good block of time for a *brain drain*. A brain drain is like stream of consciousness in writing. You simply start writing about what you want without censorship. Do not worry about spelling, grammar or presentation. With your intention to identify and list everything you want, simply allow your brain to drain. Just pour whatever is in your head out onto the paper or computer screen. Don't think too much. Just let it flow. After your initial writing session, you will most likely come back to your notebook over and over again and keep adding to it and revising what you wrote. This is because, once you've opened the door, your dreams want to keep coming through to you. And in good like-attracts-like fashion, the more you put your attention on what you want, the more you discover more of what you want. This method is simple and effective.

The way to begin is to take your notebook and create categories for your life. A three-ring binder is good because it's easy to add pages as necessary. Another style of notebook that works well is the spiral-bound that is already divided into subcategories that you can title as you wish. The key here is to give yourself plenty of space for evolution within each category. Below is a category list you can use for your brainstorming session. Or, if you wish, you can revise the list to create something more personalized:

- Physical Health & Well-Being
- Romantic Relationship
- Family Relationships
- Friendships
- Work/Career/Right Livelihood
- Finances
- Home
- Personal Growth, Goals and Achievements
- Learning/Skill Development
- Spiritual Life

Once you have established your categories, take a moment to prepare for the writing you are about to do with the following short exercise:

Read the following passage to yourself. Read it silently. Say it out loud, too. Do it several times. Let it sink in.

Your name, REMEMBER, There is Only One.
One Life, One Source, One Energy for All That Is.

That One Source is, by nature, Unconditional Love, All Good, Abundant, Perfect Health, Infinite Well-Being, Total Freedom, Harmony, Joy, Dynamic Aliveness, Direction, Clarity, Purpose, Fulfillment, Ease, Grace, All-Sufficiency, Solution, Healing, Resolution.

Because there is Only One Source for All That Is, I, too, am made up of this Source Energy and therefore embody the same qualities as it.

All I need do is ALLOW myself to want. The sky is the limit. I need only identify my heart's desires. Source Energy takes care of the rest.

As you read this to yourself a few times, do so with the intention of letting any fear, doubt, or limiting beliefs fall away. Once you become willing to access the possibility of infinite potential, start writing about what you want in your life for each category. Write while it is easy. Let it flow. Remember, don't think too much about it. If the flow doesn't happen or starts to slow down, move on to the next category. Do this for each category. Don't reread anything until you've moved through all the categories.

Two powerful results can potentially occur with the Brainstorming Method:

1.   You dare to dream to a degree that you may have never before given yourself permission to do and,

2.   You'll start to activate your wanting mechanism, and all that can follow from that. Once you've started the Brainstorming Method, it is there for you to play with and build upon in the future.

Your notebook is a wonderful tool to keep by your bedside and reread before you go to sleep. It is a powerful frame of reference for future exercises and will help immensely as you practice the remaining steps in The Formula.

Technique #4 – The Collage Method

The Collage Method is another simple yet powerful method for identifying what you want. This is a great method if you are not the verbal or writing type and/or if you enjoy arts and crafts. The Collage Method is very visual and visceral. With this method, you'll need lots of magazines that you are willing to cut up, poster board, glue sticks, scissors, and anything else that might contribute to your creative process. You will be creating a collage that captures, through imagery (and some words, if you like), your dreams – all that you desire. And you do not have to come up with a single word if you don't want to. Set aside some quality time for yourself and this project. Begin by flipping through the magazines, cutting out any images and *power* words or phrases that speak to you. You don't have to know why you like what you choose. You don't have to understand what it means. If something in you likes it, cut it out.

As you're cutting out the images and words, know that the *deeper knowing* within you is guiding you in this process. One of the reasons this process is so powerful is that it bypasses your logical mind. And believe me, your logical mind can sometimes be your worst enemy when it comes to identifying what you want. There is a part of you, your soul, which knows exactly what your dreams are. Your soul will help you identify this through the pictures you *feel* good about. If you let your desires filter through your logical mind, (or your irrational mind, for that matter), you'll often hear the "yeah but" fears, obstacles and limiting beliefs before your dream even has a chance to be heard or seen.

Once you've collected a nice pile of cutouts, start gluing them to your poster board. Watch your dream take shape through imagery and art. You can create collages for your whole life, or for one specific dream. Know that your collage can be an ongoing work in progress. Put it somewhere so you'll see it regularly and add to it as you wish. As I said, I personally use all of the techniques outlined in this section all the time. They are all fun and powerful in different ways. I always have a collage hanging in my bedroom that captures the next chapter of my life and the dreams I hold. I did a collage for my marriage and family when my husband and I were trying to conceive. I did a collage when we focused on manifesting our dream vineyard life. And then I created a collage when we wanted to create a life of wine-making, book publishing and world traveling, in a family-friendly way. It is amazingly satisfying to revisit your collage and see the things that have manifested.

Technique #5 – The Vision Workshop

The Vision Workshop is the most in-depth technique of all five for identifying what you want. This method helps you get to your soul's truth, bypassing ego-driven wants or passing fancies. I began conducting Vision Workshops back in 1995, a process I developed based on a need to gain more clarity about exactly what I wanted in a long-term relationship. I had long known I wanted a relationship but had been lost as to exactly how to define what I wanted. Through the various sources I had studied regarding relationships, I had come to discover that I wanted to define not just my dream man, but my dream relationship. I wanted to know the essence, the quality and the dynamic of this relationship – this other life form – that would come alive when my mate and I brought together our individual energies. I realized that in all the looking and wanting, I had been caught up in the *picture* – the fantasy – of it all but, without knowing the true essence of my dream relationship, I might never find true fulfillment. I had been looking for the answer but it wasn't until I found the *right questions* that I knew in my heart exactly what I wanted.

Creating a vision through the *success for the soul* model is a process of asking yourself the *right* questions – that is, the questions that will lead you to your soul's answers and to fulfillment. Without the right questions, you may very well identify wants, dreams and goals. But if you don't know yourself very well, or don't feel particularly connected to your soul's truth, you might be identifying the goals and dreams of your personality or your ego. Ego-driven goals are not necessarily a true reflection of who you really are. They are usually generated from your reactions to your upbringing, your environment, your insecurities, or your history.

The purpose and power of creating a vision for a particular dream are twofold. First, the process of creating a vision will give you crystal clarity regarding what you truly want, based in the truth of who you really are. You will actually know yourself better once you've completed a vision. And once you have completed a vision, because you will know yourself better, you will have that deeper self-awareness (and a "vision formula," so to speak) with which to create future visions. The first time you do a vision, the process may be challenging. You may be asking yourself questions you've never asked before, much less answered. You may need to engage in reflection, even ask friends for help regarding how and what they see in you. However, after you've completed this process (and sometimes it feels a little like giving birth), you will feel a new found sense of freedom, clarity and power to proactively create your life, because you will have a deeper connection to your soul and your purpose. And I promise, any vision you create thereafter will be much easier!

The second reason for doing a vision is that once it is completed, it is an incredibly powerful tool for drawing into your life exactly what you want. I can't tell you how many clients have contacted me after completing their vision to tell me of the latest miracle that happened in their life, bringing closer or actually manifesting their very dream! This stuff works if you're willing to do the work.

You may ask why this is so powerful and how exactly it works. Since like attracts like, when you don't have a clear vision, you attract all sorts of unsatisfying experiences that reflect a whole bunch of unfocused, jumbled up, and contradicting thoughts and emotions you have regarding any particular dream in your life. However, once you get clear and align your thoughts and feelings with single-minded focus (as happens when you create a vision), watch out! You have just magnified, amplified, and intensified your magnetic desire so that it can now zoom right into your life.

In this next section, you will have the opportunity to create your very own vision for a particular dream or goal in your life. The first step in creating a vision is to identify what you want to focus on. Some common areas would include your dream relationship, your dream job, your dream life or a particular life goal such as learning to play the piano, developing a healthy relationship with food and your body, living in France for a year, or being a financially free millionaire. You may know exactly what you want to focus on, or it may be a vague, hazy topic you are only now daring to consider.

In addition to getting focused, what is also important in this step is to set the tone of *infinite possibility*. This may be easy for you in that all you may need is for someone to say, "Go for it!" and you're off and running, excited at what you will discover. For others, the idea of infinite possibility brings up all sorts of obstacles. You may encounter the "Yeah buts," discouragement, evidence that supports the argument that you can't have that dream, that it will be very hard, take a long time, cost a lot of money, or you just plain don't get to have it, etc. If you fall into the second category, at this point I offer you an ultimate truth about the Universe. Read it. Read it again. Take it in. Let yourself open up to willingness – a willingness to experience the

Universe as an eternally benevolent and generous playground. If you are *willing*, anything is possible. If you are not willing to try this idea on for size, you might as well just donate this book to your local thrift shop. Here goes:

The natural state of the Universe is infinite, unlimited, lavish abundance and all you need do is LET yourself receive it.

This means that when you are not experiencing what you want in your life, it is not because, "I don't deserve it ... it's for others, but not for me ... there's not enough to go around ... I have to earn it ... I have to pay my dues ... it's not my turn." It is simply because in some way (and you will learn more about all the ways we do this) you are not letting yourself have what you want.

So, now that you're willing to open up to the infinite possibilities of having what you want, you are in the most empowering state of mind to create your vision. By the way, since we're talking about infinite possibility, I'd like to take a moment to prime the pump a little, especially if your consciousness up until now has been one of limitation and lack.

"Infinite possibilities" means you get to have what you want, without exception, and ...

- It can be easy.
- It can be effortless.
- It can happen quickly.
- You can have it now.
- You deserve it.
- There's always more than enough for everyone.
- Love and support and well-being abounds.
- It can be joyful.
- There are no conditions.

Get the idea? Good. So now let's move on to the actual process.

Exercise

I cannot emphasize enough the power of what you are about to do. The Vision Workshop activates your creative energy as if you finally plugged in a manifesting machine that you forgot you had all along.

The vision process you will engage in has four components:
1. The Springboard – Who You Dream of Becoming
2. How Your Dream Feels
3. What Your Dream Produces
4. The Purpose of Your Dream

If you were participating in the Vision Workshop, I would lead you through three guided meditations which would each be followed by a segment of quiet time for capturing in writing what you discovered during your meditations. The fourth component of the vision workshop is an exercise that helps you get really clear and really specific about who you are. Once you've completed the four components, then you have within you and in front of you the information you need to create a distilled, clear, focused vision for your dream.

The Difference between a Vision and Goals

If you are familiar with goal setting, you may be asking, "Why should I engage in such an in-depth process to define what I want? I know what I want. As a matter of fact, I've got my goals right here." Well, when you list goals, it's possible to fall into the trap of having no more than a checklist of "to do" items, which even if achieved, leave you still yearning or longing for some elusive something that will make you happy. Goals are better left for action strategies. And action strategies come *after* you create a vision. A vision, on the other hand, gets you in touch with who you want and need to *be*. A vision works from the inside out, so that you're internally driven and focused on your desire as opposed to being externally driven. When you are internally driven, your soul is in the driver's seat. Your heart, your gut, your intuition take over the navigational system for your life, and this will keep you on course. If you are externally driven, you are usually being enticed, tempted or pulled in any number of different directions. You are basically *reacting* to your environment, whether it's the media, well-meaning friends, parents or the supreme court that lives in your head (fueled by a list of 'shoulds' your parents or community handed you growing up). When you let your external world take over your navigational system, it is very hard to know if you are on course and it is easy to feel lost and confused.

So, although it may be challenging to create a vision and ask questions you have never asked or answered before, in doing so, you will awaken and activate your internal navigational system. The feeling of freedom, empowerment and possibility that comes with this is beyond compare.

The Process

Since your vision writing process will be in a workbook format as opposed to a workshop format, the process will be a little different but no less effective. I'd encourage you to set aside some quiet time dedicated to getting clear about your dream and I recommend that you work on this one component at a time. Thirty to 60 minutes at each sitting would be very productive, or you can lock yourself in a cabin for a weekend and really give yourself to this process – whatever works for you. The main thing is that you want to create some quiet, uninterrupted time. You might want to light a candle or hit a gong three times before you start, to symbolically create sacred space and shift gears from your normal life. You might want to take a few breaths with your eyes closed. Do whatever works for you and your body to know that this is time for you to connect with you – the real you, the bigger you – your soul.

By the way, this is a good time to let you in on an important aspect of this process and that is, *there is no right way to do this*. It could be very easy to get caught up in doing it right, or getting attached to a particular outcome. That kind of thinking is the kind that is externally driven. This book offers guidelines, ideas, inspirations and possibilities. But, hey! If you aren't the verbal or writing kind, and after reviewing the questions, you draw a picture and know without a doubt *that* is your vision, THEN *that* is your vision. Trust yourself. Trust your heart. Trust your gut. Your emotional reactions will consistently reveal valuable information about your soul's truth. If you get caught up in *doing it right,* then your head is taking over and I'll tell you right now, when it comes to making dreams come true, logic and reason can often hurt more than help. The vision process is a journey of opening up to a deeper wisdom and different kinds of intelligence.

What You Will Need

To create your vision you will need the following:
- An attitude of willingness and openness to infinite possibilities.
- Quiet, uninterrupted time and space.
- Paper and pen or a computer.

The Springboard

The first component to your vision work is designed to open you up to thinking about your dream from the most expansive place possible. Many times, when we think about a dream that we have, the very first thoughts that pop into our minds are the perceived obstacles. Let's say your dream is to have a fulfilling relationship. Your first thoughts might be in the realm of: "Those kinds of relationships only happen in the movies ... the only good men out there are married or gay ... all women these days are ball-busters ... I'm just a 'bad relationship magnet' ... it can't happen for me ... I have no idea how to have a successful relationship ... I have too many issues ... I'm damaged goods ... I'm not pretty enough ... I'm too old ... I'm bald ... overweight, etc."

Or maybe you have the dream of a fulfilling career, *but* "... I'd have to go back to school and it is too expensive and will take forever ... I can't afford to look for another job, my family depends on me ... I want to do something completely different but don't know where to begin, etc."

Maybe you want to successfully release excess weight and keep it off once and for all *but* "... I have no will power ... I've failed a million times ... I'm destined to be fat."

The purpose of Component #1 is to create a springboard, a launching pad from which you can bypass all the perceived limitation. **Know this: When you do a vision, you are not thinking about how it is going to happen. The only thing to think about is WHAT you want.** Your mission is to uncover your desire in Technicolor, virtual reality detail. The rest will follow.

So, Component #1 is designed to open you up so that when you begin answering the three questions that will follow, you will be answering them from a place of the infinite possibility of who you want to be in your life. Here we go …

COMPONENT #1 – Reflect upon and write about the following: Who do you dream of becoming?

Allow yourself to travel back in time to when you were a child. Allow yourself to connect with who you were, what was important to you, the people around you, your environment. Begin moving forward in time, gathering together thoughts, feelings, memories and images of your life – the positive and the negative. Reflect on the experiences that have contributed to who you are today – relationships, events, environments, your wants, wishes and dreams. Spend as much time as you need to reconnect with your history, and the individual threads that have been woven into the fabric of who you are today.

Once you feel complete with the past, feel yourself move forward in time to when you are an old person. See and feel yourself as this old person. Imagine yourself to be blissfully content doing whatever you are doing. As this person, imagine yourself reflecting back on your life in a state of utter contentment, completely fulfilled by the life you've lived and the person you've become. Allow yourself to connect with what that life would be – your relationships, your work, your leisure time, your hobby, your community – everything. Imagine the life that would allow you to reflect back with absolutely no regrets.

Once you feel complete with this, feel yourself gathering together everything you have discovered for yourself and bring it all back into the present moment. Now take some time to write about all that you connected with. Remember, there is no right way to do this. Let this be a stream of consciousness. Let go of all judgment and all concerns of anyone ever reading this, grammar, spelling, etc. **Write about the person you dream of becoming.**

COMPONENT #2 – *Reflect upon and write about the following: How does living your dream* feel?

In this next section you will be exploring many of the intangibles of what it would be like to be living your dream.

Allow yourself to imagine that somehow, magically, you have transcended all time and space. All the obstacles you ever thought might stand between you and your dream have vanished. And, at this very moment, right NOW, you are living your dream. Take a few deep breaths to *imagine* what that would *feel* like right now.

If your dream is to be a financially free multimillionaire, *feel* what that would feel like. Imagine you just put away your checkbook and *see* the balance you would like to see. Imagine you just opened your most recent portfolio statement. *Feel* the paper between your fingers and *see* the numbers printed on the page that represents your wealth. *Feel* what it would feel like to have all of your debts and financial responsibilities paid in full, to know that all of your businesses are operating at an ever-increasing profit, to know that your personal income allows you to live, play, invest and give to your heart's content.

If your dream is be a published author, *feel* what it would feel like to hold your published book in your hands. Open the book up and inhale the smell of the new ink on the paper. *Imagine* yourself standing in a bookstore and seeing before you on the shelf your book with your title and your name on it. *See* yourself in a radio studio being interviewed about your book and *hear* the questions that readers are calling in with to the radio show.

These are just examples to prime the pump, so to speak. The main idea is to *feel* the reality of your dream experience right now. Once you are connected with that, allow yourself to explore further what it would feel like for you to be living your dream. **Write about the qualities, the essence, and the intangible feelings you would experience living your dream.**

COMPONENT #3 – *Reflect upon and write about the following: What does your dream produce?*

In this next section, you will explore what living your dream will produce for you personally, for your loved ones, and for what I call "the world at large." Another way to look at this is to acknowledge that living your dream will produce results, both tangible and intangible.

Imagine again you are living your dream. Allow yourself to connect with what that will produce for you personally. What are the tangible things you will be able to see, hear, taste, touch and smell. What will you have that you didn't have before? What will you have achieved that you hadn't achieved before? On an intangible level, who will you have become, what will your life be an example of? Spend some time really exploring this for yourself.

Next, take some time to connect with what living your dream will produce for your loved ones. No matter how important or invisible we may think we are in the world, we *all* affect others; there is no escaping that. When you're not living your dream, you're affecting others. When you are living your dream, you are affecting others. Take some time now to imagine how those you love most will be affected by you living your dream. What tangible results will they experience as a result? Tangibles tend to be easier because they are the *things* of life – a house, a car, a good education.

Intangibles can be a bit trickier but just as important. What intangible things will they perceive? If, for example, you're exploring what your dream relationship will produce for your loved ones, you may want to start with how your dream relationship will affect your mate. Intangibles here might be something such as:

- A safe place for him to discover and express who he wants to be in the world.
- The knowledge that he is loved and accepted for exactly who he is.
- A reason to be his best.

Let's say your dream is to be a successful Broadway actor. The intangible results your loved ones might experience may include:

- Proof that dreams really can come true.
- Firsthand exposure to the exciting world of theatre and the arts.

- Having a dad who comes home feeling fully alive and with much more to give.

Once you've spent some time exploring what your dream will produce for your loved ones, then spend some time exploring what living your dream will produce for the world at large. The phrase "the world at large" does not necessarily need to be taken literally. The world at large for you might be your neighbors, your community or your workplace. Then again, you might want to live your life at a global level and then the world at large truly is the world at large. What I mean by "the world at large" speaks to the fact that, once again, we all affect people around us. We affect people everyday in ways we don't even realize. This book, for example, will hopefully affect the lives of many people around the world whom I will never meet. When you are *not* living your dream, there might be a thread of discontent that runs through everything you do. You never know how a more fulfilled *you* might actually be a pivotal turning point one day in the life of a store clerk you spoke to while you were feeling full of life, joy and gratitude.

So, in acknowledgment of this fact, take some time to write about what you living your dream will produce for the world at large. For example:

- A neighborhood mom who all the kids know they can count on for a smile, a warm hug and cookies.
- An example to friends and family that a successful and fulfilling marriage really is possible.
- A dose of inspiration in a world that is bombarded by "bad news" at every turn.

COMPONENT #4 – What is the purpose of your dream?

Your goal in this component of your vision work is to distill everything you are about to do into **one sentence, maybe two**. This process will be different than the first three components because, instead of free-flowing journaling, you will engage in a three-step process that builds upon itself. By the end of this process, you will arrive at:

- ONE sentence that declares your purpose in life, and
- ONE sentence that declares the purpose of your dream.

This next section is what I call the *Why* of your dream. It is the reason, the purpose, that fuels the birth and life of your dream. The important thing to know about this particular *Why* is that it goes deep, to the soul of who you are. If you don't identify the real and true reason for your dream, it will be all too easy to give up on it when times get tough. The true *Why* of your dream will be a reflection of who you are (as opposed to a more superficial personality or ego-driven desire). And so, in order to get to the true purpose of your dream, you must know the true purpose of *you*.

This may seem daunting, for I am asking you nothing less than "What is the meaning of life to you?" Ah yes, an age-old question pondered by many a great philosopher. Well, the good news is that there's a fun and fascinating way to arrive at your answer. This component is more of a thinking process. You may even benefit from enlisting the help of your friends. This process can sometimes feel a bit like giving birth. But, oh boy, when that baby pops out – i.e. your purpose statement – watch out! You'll be running around yelling, "I know who I am and I know my purpose!" Once you know your purpose, identifying the purpose of your dream will be relatively easy. You will never again *not* know what you know – that means *you*. So, you will never again be able to just want for the sake of wanting. The satisfaction of wanting for wanting's sake will pale in contrast to *desiring* for your soul's authentic need to express itself!

So, here goes. Are you ready to discover the meaning of life to you and hence the purpose of your dream? Let's go ...

Step #1 - Identify the character that you are.
If I were to ask you, "What's the meaning of life to you?" you may just grunt, "Huh?" Too big a question. You are in the forest too deeply to see the trees. However, by creating some distance from yourself and your life, you get a whole new perspective. So the question now becomes:

"If you were a character in a book, what type of character would you be?"

The way to figure this out is to stand back and think about how you look at the world. What kinds of glasses do you view life with? What really excites you and turns you on? For example, when I posed this question to myself, I became clear that I look at the world as a student of life. I'm a student and a teacher. I'm passionate about seeing what I can learn about life, and just as passionate about sharing my discoveries with others. I later realized that I'm also an artist or creator. These are the characters that capture how I *do* life. Take a look at the list of characters below and mark the ones that speak to you – the ones that resonate for you, that make you think, "Hmm, this might be me."

Student	Singer	Teacher	Actor
Priestess	Artist	Astronaut	Comedian
Adventurer	Leader	Healer	Engineer
Dancer	Mother	Wife	Builder
Nurturer	Warrior	Athlete	Cowboy
Musician	Facilitator	Minister	Seer
Cruise Director	Child	Explorer	Pioneer
Sociologist	Champion	Producer	Creator
Goddess	Coach		

Once you've gravitated to the ones that feel like you, begin to narrow them down. You will need to pick **no more than three characters**. If you can't narrow them down to three, then you need to come up with a new character. (This, by the way, is how this list grew. In each Vision Workshop, there would inevitably be participants who would come up with new characters because they couldn't find **their** character on the list.)

Next – Once you've got your character, start listing the VERBS – the actions or ways of being – the character engages in.

For example:
- **Student:** learns, analyzes, observes, experiences, digests, assimilates, explores, dissects, reflects upon, researches, studies ...
- **Teacher:** teaches, imparts, inspires, synthesizes, distills, exemplifies, models, stimulates
- **Creator:** creates, designs, formulates, produces, makes, expresses, contributes, beautifies, blends, offers ....

These *verbs* are very important, for they are the energies, the activities, the creative expression you engage in when you are being YOU, fully expressed, fully engaged, fully alive. Notice how different words make you feel. Notice the words, the verbs that activate that special something inside your gut. That feeling is your soul saying, "Yeah! That's IT. That's ME. That's what I'm here to do!"

Helpful Hint

If you're struggling with this section and haven't been able to identify or narrow down your character(s) and your verbs, enlist the help of friends or family who know you well. You may be surprised at how clearly they see you, or even HOW they see you. This process may be easy or it may be difficult. Give yourself the time and energy to get clarity about you. Even if you have to step away and come back to this exercise, don't quit on it. Like I said, it's a little like giving birth, but when you know who you are, YOU KNOW WHO YOU ARE!

Step #2 – Identify the meaning of life for you as that character.

Now that you've narrowed down the characters you are and the verbs you engage in, start exploring the specifics of how and what you do with those verbs.

For example:

When I engaged in this process, I asked myself, "Okay, I'm a student and a teacher, but a student and a teacher of what?" After some reflection, I came to realize I am a student and a teacher of all things having to do with God and spirituality. And I got further clarity when I identified that God and spirituality are all about *love* to me. So, I realized that the meaning of life to me as a student and a teacher was to "experience, learn and teach how to live life through love ... how to see everything in life through the eyes of love, and how to be guided in my actions through a context of love."

Here are a few more examples:

Artist: One workshop participant, who identified her character as 'artist,' defined her truly engaging verbs as *expressing* beauty and *seeing* the beauty in all things.

Wife: Another participant saw herself as 'wife.' Now she was not actually married, but all the ways she would describe the way she approached life was aligned with how she would define the character of 'wife.' So, the meaning of life for her was to *support, nurture, partner* and *encourage* others towards their success.

Special Note about Characters

It is important to understand that **just because you might fulfill a certain role in your life, and do it well, does NOT mean that it's your character!** Just because you are a wife and mother does NOT necessarily mean that either of those are your characters. I, for example, am both, but those are not my characters. I also had a workshop participant who had a tough time shaking off the role she played in life as a wife because she was so good at it. But luckily, her friend was doing the workshop with her and she said, "Oh my gosh! You're a *total* artist, girlfriend! Everything you say, do and think about is in this really creative way!" This participant had a hard time owning the 'artist' character she was because, up until that point, she wasn't doing anything *artist-like* in her life. But when she finally let herself feel 'artist' in her gut, she realized how enlivening it was for her. By the way, an 'artist' character may never actually choose to *be* an artist, but may approach life as an artist, in a creative, expressive sort of way. For example, one of my characters is 'artist/creator,' and although I do not often engage in artistic endeavors, my artistic medium is, "*creating* sacred spaces for people to discover, experience and express their true Selves, through being, reflecting and relating."

Step #3 - Formulating your purpose statement(s)

Once you've identified your character(s) and verbs, and explored more in depth how you express those in your life, it becomes time to hone and clarify your purpose statement for your life. Once you've got your purpose statement for your life, you will have it forever as a powerful tool to draw upon in the manifestation of any dream or goal. Here are a few guidelines to help you arrive at this all powerful, single sentence:

1. You will begin with, "The purpose of my life is to _____."
2. You will follow with at least one verb, and then other clarifying information, which will most likely include more of your favorite verbs.
3. You will end with a period.

These guidelines may sound silly to you, but trust me on this. I'm going to *push* you to come up with *one sentence*. I'm telling you, I've seen people jump up in the air and hoot and holler when their sentence came together. There is an unbelievable sense of freedom, power and knowing that comes from having the purpose for your life stare you back in the face from a piece of paper. **And you will know when it is right, because it will feel just right.** Let's break it down ...

"The purpose of my life is to _____."
So, how exactly do you fill in the blank? This is where those verbs come in handy. Go back to your list of verbs and highlight the ones that vibrate in your gut.

Here is a list to help get you started:
The purpose of my life is to...
* provide ...
* deliver ...
* learn ...
* experience ...
* exemplify ...
* create ...
* produce ...
* leave behind ...
* nurture ...
* engage in the process ...
* help ...
* contribute ...

Go back to those explorations about what you do with those verbs and highlight those words. *Words are powerful.* They are energy. They are creative. They *do* vibrate. And when the vibration of the words matches the vibration of your soul, you will feel it. Start playing around with the words. Make it a game. Move things around. And definitely enlist the help of friends. You'll feel it when your statement is getting close. You'll feel the words that are not quite right. Just keep playing around with them. And if it isn't coming together, step away for a while and revisit it. You'd be amazed how your unconscious will go to work for you and simply send you the *right answer* at another time.

Examples of Life Purpose Statements
- *The purpose of my life is to stoke the engine of personal creative expression by encouraging and awakening in others the divine right to a finely honed, passionate life.*
- *The purpose of my life is to be an example of a woman who fully embraces life.*
- . *The purpose of my life is to engage in the process of locating and expressing my fullest potential as a human being.*
- *The purpose of my life is to inspire others to open their hearts to their passions through music.*
- *The purpose of my life is to contribute to a better world by creating uniquely splendid objets d'art that make people happy.*

Creating a Purpose Statement for Your Dream
Once you know the purpose for your life, creating a purpose statement for your dream will be much easier. Again, your dream will be a reflection of the meaning of life to you. Think about it: "If your dream does not contribute to that which gives your life meaning, why would you pursue it?" This is a powerful question to ponder. For, if you cannot identify how the pursuit of your dream contributes to a meaningful life, you may want to reflect upon why exactly you are expending your energy in this direction.

Soul Desire vs. Personality-Driven Wanting
There is a big difference between a desire that comes from deep within your soul and the wantings or passing fancies of your personality or ego. The more you get to know the deeper you, the more you will be able to distinguish the difference simply by how the longing feels. You may have gathered by now that in this

book we aren't going to be putting much attention or energy into personality-driven wantings. Two important reasons why are:

1. Although you may truly think you want what your personality wants, even if you reach your goal, it won't be satisfying for very long. You will most likely experience a short-lived "Yahoo!" quickly followed by that antsy feeling that there should be more. Since *my* soul's desire is to help you feel as fully free and satisfied in and with your life as possible, we are going to go beyond the *Yahoo!* into the territory of *more*.

2. As for being effective in the successful pursuit of your dreams, pursuing from your personality is much less effective than pursuing from the depths of your soul. One reason is that when you pursue dreams or goals from your ego, you are seeking from a context of lack. (For more on *ego* refer to Chapter 15.) In other words, I don't have *this*, therefore I want *it*. And, manifesting something from lack is exponentially more difficult than creating from abundance. When you pursue a dream from your soul, the context from which you are creating is abundance, i.e., *already having-ness*. ("This is who I AM. This is what I HAVE within me, and I must *express* this in my life.")

Now, I'm not saying you can't successfully pursue a goal that was birthed as a result of some external or seemingly superficial reason. What I'm saying is, the reason or **purpose** for this dream in your life must be framed as something that is aligned with your soul's desire for expressing the full potential of *you* in your life. Otherwise, your soul will get antsy and will keep bugging you until you listen. A reason for your dream that would keep your self-expression smaller than your soul longs for would *not* be very effective.

A good and common example is in the realm of weight loss: Plenty of folk have been compelled to *want* to lose extra weight for external or personality-driven reasons – "I want to look good for my class reunion," "I want to look like that supermodel," "I want Jane or John to find me attractive." These are all good motivators to help you identify the desire but the truth is, these reasons won't keep you going for the long-haul. You may indeed lose weight for your class reunion, or get to the point where you look like a supermodel, or become more attractive to Jane or John. However, what happens after you achieve that? Chances are good you'll gain the weight back because nothing changed in terms of you expressing the full potential of YOU. So, the trick would be to expand and deepen your context for losing weight so that it satisfies your soul's longing for more authentic self-expression.

Are you a 'student/teacher' character? Then your purpose for losing weight could have something to do with *learning* to take better care of yourself as a way of being more loving toward yourself and *teaching* your children by example.

Are you an 'adventurer' character? Then your purpose for losing weight could have something to do with *taking the necessary risks* to let go of old patterns and *discover* a healthier, more empowered you! Get the idea?

A Personal Anecdote

As long as I can remember, I wanted to get married, have children and live happily ever after. I knew all the fairy tales and bought into them hook, line and sinker. Like many a girl growing through her adolescence, I had my share of exhilarating and painful crushes on boys. I watched wistfully as other girls had boyfriends and I "wanted one." If you'd asked me why then, I couldn't have told you. As I grew into young adulthood, these longings, without deeper awareness, continued to pull at me. I longed. I wanted. I wished. So much so, that in my mid-twenties, I started seeing a metaphysical counselor who called herself a *community yentl*. She taught the art of *attracting and keeping a lifetime mate*. So, I started seeing her and she turned me on to a teacher and a body of work that educated me on the subject of male–female relationships and how to create successful ones.

I studied with that teacher and that organization for ten years. I thought of it as my Ph.D. course in relationships. It was during this self-discovery period that I realized I wanted to get married but had no idea why. The truth was, I was afraid of men and didn't trust them. And frankly, I didn't like them very much. Kind of a strange paradox, wouldn't you say? So, when I discovered *this* truth, my focus changed from wanting some elusive dream relationship with a man, to wanting to heal my relationships with all men. And I did. After a few years of determinedly identifying and healing my wounds and perceptions regarding relationships with men, I reached a point where I felt free. I had learned to like and accept myself. I had learned to like and accept men. All those holes I was looking to men to fill had been filled by *me* and my relationship with *me*. I then knew I could bring a whole person to a relationship rather than someone needing to be completed by another.

So, here I was, wanting a relationship with a man, but now I knew *why* even less. And then it dawned on me, if I was going to commit my life to another human being and make the sacrifices I would need to make to sustain a relationship for the rest of my life, this relationship had better darned well have something to offer me that nothing else in life could. I realized marriage was a unique life experience unto itself. I realized marriage could offer opportunities for living, loving and growing that nothing else could – not work, not family, not leisure, not hobbies, not school, not friendship. Nowhere else did a life experience call upon me to choose another human being with whom to create fulfillment for a lifetime.

I thought, "This is heavy duty stuff, so I'd better find out why the heck I'd want to do this." In other words, I knew too well that times can get tough in a marriage. I, like everyone else, had plenty of evidence of this. Even in the best of family circumstances, people lose their jobs, have money challenges, children are tempted by unsafe and undesirable situations, people get sick, people get bored. That is, life happens.

I started to ask myself some really hard questions, such as: "What are the conditions I put on my commitment to a long-term relationship?" In other words, "I'm committed to you for the rest of my life *until* _____." (Here is where you fill in the blanks – *you cheat on me ... we go bankrupt ... you won't help around the house, etc. "If I choose to get married, what will keep me going through the hard times? What would be the* reason?

What would be the higher purpose *that would keep me going when my worst fears happened, when I couldn't remember why I got married in the first place?"* I realized if I was going to put conditions on my commitment, then I shouldn't get married. For better or for worse, meant for better or for WORSE!

In other words, if this is really my dream, then I'd better make sure it really is my dream – that I really want THIS not THAT. I also need to know what the deeper, soul purpose for my dream is. That which will allow me to experience the true fulfillment of it.

It was with this awakening that I realized some biggies about marriage dreams specifically, and life dreams in general. You can find more guidance for specific dreams like marriage, work, food & body, prosperity, etc., in the Recommended Resources section in the appendix of this book or at:
www.successforthesoul.com.

Once you've let yourself want what you want, do yourself the favor of really exploring your want to see if you really do want that thing or if you want something else, something deeper. Do you want to lose weight, or do you really want to feel confident about yourself and you think losing weight will help you accomplish that? Do you want to write a book, or do you want the experience of touching people's lives with what you have learned? Do you want a man with money, or are you really looking for the safety and security you think money will bring? Do you want to get married, or do you *not* want to feel lonely (these are two very different things). The Vision Workshop process will help you go deeper and get clear about your dreams.

Back to Purpose Statements
So now that you have more context for the purpose of your dream, it's time to come up with the purpose statement for your dream. Remember those characters, verbs and life purpose statements. Now it is time to take all you've discovered and see how your dream will give you the opportunity to experience and express that which gives your life meaning. Use the modified guidelines below:

- Start with, "The purpose of (state your dream here) is to
  _____."
- Fill in the blank with the meaty stuff.
- End with a period.

Below are some purpose statements for dreams to help you
in your process. You may want to take notice of the verbs and see
if you can tell which characters inspired the purpose statement.

Relationship and Marriage
- *The purpose of my relationship is to learn about life
  through experiences and discoveries that are shared with
  my partner.*
- *The purpose of our relationship is to build a family where
  our children grow up believing in themselves and knowing that they are loved.*
- *The purpose of our relationship is to co-create a fully free
  and prosperous life by experiencing and expressing the
  infinite power of love!*

Work and Career
- *The purpose of our partnership is to provide XYZ Micro-
  systems with superior consulting services as a united
  team, so that XYZ always thinks of us first and is incredibly satisfied with our work.*
- *The purpose of my dream career is to help others realize
  the power they have to be, do and have all they can imagine and more.*
- *The purpose of making the sacrifices necessary to write
  my novel is to exemplify to my children that life is a trea-
  sure and we have a responsibility to go after our dreams.*
- *The purpose of my artwork is to nurture the dream of a
  global village by educating people about the richness and
  beauty of other cultures and traditions.*

Money and Prosperity
- *The purpose of my dream for prosperity is to experience
  and express the freedom and power to live and give without limitation.*

- *The purpose of my financial freedom is to give my children the opportunities I wish I'd had.*
- *The purpose of my financial abundance is to give me the time to be more available to my family.*

Creating Your Vision

You have now completed all four components of the Vision Workshop:

1. The person you dream of becoming.
2. The "How" of your dream.
3. The "What" of your dream.
4. The "Why" of your dream.

It's now time to distill everything you've discovered into your vision for your dream.

Remember: There is no right way to do this! Trust yourself and your process. However, I do have some guidelines that may be helpful. You will be weaving together aspects of your *How,* your *What* and your *Why* to create your vision. The *Person You Dream of Becoming* will already be incorporated naturally into your vision because, as you may recall, the reason for beginning this process with that exercise was to create a springboard for allowing infinite possibility into your consciousness. Some visions turn out to be a few sentences. Other visions are a few paragraphs. Some are pictures (a real demonstration that you trust yourself and your process). Some turn out to be one sentence. As a matter of fact, some people feel so clear and empowered once they identify their *Why* statement that one sentence becomes their vision.

The "Cut and Paste" Method

One way to begin distilling all you have discovered is to go back over what you wrote for your *How, What* and *Why* and begin highlighting what feels most important. If you wrote on your computer, you can literally cut and paste favorite words and phrases together to create your masterpiece. You may very well discover in this process that there is quite a bit of repetition in what you wrote. Repetition is good because it means your soul keeps coming back to, and expressing, that which is most important to you. Once you've highlighted what speaks to you most, then you can begin piecing things together in an order or flow that feels right. This is *your* vision. Have fun with it. Try different things on for size. You'll know when it feels right.

The "Sleep On It" Method

I discovered this method because the *Cut and Paste* method didn't work for me. Try as I may, I couldn't get anything to flow from stringing together the bits and pieces I had highlighted during my own vision process. So, after reading over my writings, rereading them, highlighting, moving things around and ultimately feeling sufficiently fed up, I put everything away for a while. Then when I was ready to revisit my vision, I simply sat down and started writing and out it came! The reason this works is that your subconscious mind is a powerful force. It is busy at work even when you don't realize it. Your subconscious mind stores, processes, digests, integrates and creates on your behalf. So, letting it all go and coming back to it, really does work.

Progress vs. Perfection

Your goal in the Vision Workshop is to arrive at what I call *a working version* of your vision. Even if it doesn't feel *perfect,* give yourself the opportunity to create a vision that is *good enough.* You'll be amazed at what you start to draw into your life simply by having gone through the process of gaining clarity for yourself, even if you don't yet have all the answers. *Any* vision is better than *no* vision because:

- Remember, you are a magnet and like attracts like. If, up until now, you have been unclear and contradictory about what you want in your life, that will be what you've been attracting – unclear and contradicting manifestations. When you have a vision, even if it's a work in progress, you are now putting out what you want in your life with more focus and will easily and naturally begin attracting what you want with that much more power.
- In the process of attracting more of what you want, anything you *don't* want will become magnified or more noticeable. A working version of your vision then becomes

a powerful tool in continuing to clarify what you want. As you clarify more of what you want, you'll be able to continue revising your vision until you feel complete.

Sally's Story

Sally's experience with her vision illustrated the above point with great potency. She had completed a vision for the relationship of her dreams after attending the Vision Workshop, and shortly thereafter drew into her life the most wonderful man she had ever met. They developed a romantic relationship and dated for the better part of a year. He was everything she ever wanted. Eventually, though, he ended the relationship. And as she reflected upon what she had with him, and the vision she had created, she realized she had neglected to include a critical desire within her vision. Sally told me, "Sonia, he was everything I wanted in a man, but I wasn't everything he wanted in a woman. I realized that my vision includes mutual adoration!" She revised her vision to include this and, shortly thereafter, Sally met her future husband. She is now happily married with a baby boy.

Please note: You need not worry about spelling out every last detail of what you want ad nauseam. Sally could have just as easily attracted a relationship of mutual adoration without spelling it out in her vision. The Universe picks up your *vibration* whether you verbalize it or not, whether you are conscious of it or not. Sally's story simply illustrates how, even if your vision doesn't feel final or perfect or complete when you start, any vision is definitely better than no vision. Your vision can catapult you into a deeper understanding of who you want to be to create fulfillment with your dream. Sally discovered that there were still places in her where she could grow regarding her capacity to receive love. And when she realized the lack of it in her relationship, she grew quickly to allow herself to have it.

More Vision Writing Guidelines

- Focus on the essence and the form will come.
- State everything in the present tense.

- State everything in the positive.

When you focus on the essence and allow the form to come, you are removing your preconceived ideas about how your dream should look and letting the Universe give you the best possible version of your dream. So, if you are visioning about money, you'll want to focus on the *essence* of prosperity vs. some magic number, let's say $1,000,000. When you are visioning about romantic relationships, you'll want to focus on how your dream relationship with a woman would *feel* vs. fixating on a particular gal, let's say Betty. When you are visioning about a new living situation, you'll want to focus on the essence of your dream home, rather than becoming attached to 31 Pinecone Lane.

But here's the caveat: You actually *can* focus on $1,000,000, or Betty, or 31 Pinecone Lane, *as long as you can feel good while you are doing it.* The Universe matches your vibration. And the only thing that matters is how you *feel* when you are focusing on your dream. The reason I discourage you from focusing on the form when creating your vision is that you might get *attached* to the form. When this happens, it can be a slippery slope into the land of *feel bad.* And when this is your vibration, the Universe will manifest for you the experience of feeling bad. For example, sometimes if we get attached to a particular form, we'll perceive lack or scarcity when it doesn't manifest exactly according to our image. Or, when you expect your dream to look a certain way over here, you might miss another better opportunity over there. You might have been pining away for Betty, and missed Julia altogether.

As for stating everything in the positive, you must remember that the Universe manifests whatever has your attention. So, if in your vision for prosperity you state, "We don't have debt," the Universe doesn't hear "don't." It hears that your attention is on debt. The same principle applies to stating everything in the present tense. If you state, "I *will* weigh 135 pounds," then the Universe will manifest you being in a state of *someday this will happen.* If you state, "I weigh 135 pounds," the Universe gives you that!

What to Do With Your Vision

Congratulations! You've completed your vision and you should be very proud. Not only do you have laser focus clarity about what you want, but you should now know yourself better than before. All of this empowers the vibration of your intention into the Universe. As a result you will see a new level of manifestation in your life. Your next step now is to find a way to honor your vision. Type it up. Frame it. Decorate it if you like. The more attention and intention you infuse your vision with, the more magnetic it becomes within you. There is a lot of power in reading your vision with feeling every day. Give copies to special trusted friends so they can hold your vision with you and for you.

Final Thoughts on Step I

By now you should have a pretty good idea of the importance of knowing what you want. The opportunity lies in enjoying your desires, whether they have manifested or not. Have fun identifying what you want. Play with the dissonance that life gives you. Play with the techniques. But above all else, PLAY! If you're sick of the long, grey winter, rather than complain, see it as an opportunity to declare to yourself your love of sunshine and your intention to have more of it in your life. Your Wanting Mechanism is available to you all the time. Your power lies in whether you allow your mechanism to fuel your dissatisfaction or catapult you towards your dreams. Let your dislikes remind you of your desires. And let your desires pull you into their world.

Now, on to Step II of The Mystic's Formula!

THE MYSTIC'S FORMULA
Step II:

Pretend You Already Have It

8

Motivational vs. Metaphysical

"The thing always happens that you really believe in;
and the belief in a thing makes it happen."

— *Frank Lloyd Wright (1867-1959)*
renowned American architect

Once you know what you want, the generally accepted philosophy is to *go out and get it*. However, I'm going to offer you an alternative approach. Once you know what you want, *pretend you already have it*. That's right! Fake it till you make it. Although this notion could easily be dismissed as fluff, empty cheerleading, or an overused cliché, do not underestimate the power of these words. *Pretend You Already Have It* embodies a timeless mystical wisdom that escapes many. For those it has not escaped, it has been taught, described and explained in numerous ways. *Pretend You Already Have It* is not a new idea, yet it loses absolutely no power in repetition. Pretending you already have it allows you to access the magic, the power and the infinite potential of Divine Intelligence. You may never fully understand how it works, but if you are smart, you'll learn how to use the fact that it does. Like the law of gravity or the existence of electricity, it exists and you may not fully understand how it works, but you use it to your advantage every day of your life.

Step I of The Formula, *Identify What You Want,* is a common first step in most approaches to success. At Step II, however, you are now being presented with a choice. You can either walk toward your dream or you can fly toward it. Doesn't flying sound like a lot more fun? If you choose to walk toward your dream, you approach it with a *go out and get it* attitude, or the motivational approach. This approach can and does work, but it is just that – work. If, however, you'd rather fly (i.e., have more fun, get there faster and be uplifted by a force and power greater than your own), you'll spend some time learning about the science, the magic and the power of *Pretending You Have It* – the metaphysical approach. Of course, the obvious answer is, "Okay. I'm game. Tell me about this pretending thing." But before we get into that, I'd like to explain a little bit more about the difference between motivational and metaphysical. This understanding will allow you to use Step II with that much more power.

First know this: Both methods work. One is not the *right* one and the other the *wrong* one. They simply offer different things and fit better for different people depending on their nature and preferences. A motivational approach to success reflects a common collective consciousness which values *action* above all else. Some may think of it as a school of thought. Some may think of it as reflective of the American culture. Whatever its origin, a motivational approach encourages, supports and teaches a whole lot of *doing.* A person using the tools inherent in a motivational approach to success draws heavily upon a mental and therefore logical analysis of the conditions they are dealing with, as well as the physical realm of strategizing and executing action plans. They rely on their own will, their own mind, and their own power. Although there is room for emotional and spiritual wisdom here, it tends to be secondary.

A metaphysical approach to success assumes a deep understanding of the power and purpose of *being.* A metaphysical approach still uses the mental and physical expressions of pursuing success. Yet, the deeper resources accessible through spiritual and emotional channels are primary in the process. A discipline of *being* open, receptive and trusting of a divine intelligence – which is understood to be all-loving, all-wise, and all-powerful – takes priority over action, action, action first. Action is, of course, pivotal to the metaphysical process, but it becomes *inspired* action. All action is fueled and guided by this grander force, like the wind beneath the bird's wings.

A motivational approach to the inevitable obstacles that will arise when we pursue our dreams can lend itself to *skipping over* or *getting over* the emotional challenges. (An example of this would be approaching weight loss as a matter of will power without supporting a deeper level of empowerment and understanding at the emotional and psychological levels.) A metaphysical approach *meets* the obstacles by honoring and harnessing the power of all the feelings that show up when we are going for our dreams. This is done through understanding that it is in allowing the emotional energy to move, that the deeper, soulful guidance becomes available to us.

Another way to understand the difference between motivational and metaphysical approaches to success lies in referring to the yin yang symbol:

The symbol originates in ancient Chinese philosophy and metaphysics. It denotes two opposing but complementary forces found throughout the Universe. It represents wholeness and harmony and also reflects duality and balance. Yin is the darker element, feminine, passive, representing the night and the intuitive. Yang is the brighter element, masculine, active, representing the day and the analytical. A motivational approach relies heavily on traditionally masculine qualities, i.e., *find* out what you want, *make* your goals, *do* a strategy, *develop* a time line, keep *taking actions*, *go out* and *get it*. A metaphysical approach incorporates some of this, but also accesses the power based in traditionally feminine qualities as well, i.e., *be still*, *open* up, *allow a space* to *listen* and *receive* guidance from your soul (your intuition) as to what you want, *let* a vision of your desire *reveal* itself, *surrender* to the images and the feelings that you would experience if you already had your dream, *allow* it to come to you. Did you notice a difference in the words, especially the verbs, used to describe the two approaches?

Find, Make, Do, Develop, Take Action, Go Out, Get

vs.

Be Still, Open, Allow a Space, Listen, Receive, Let, Reveal, Surrender

These words feel pretty different when you read them, don't they?

To understand and use Step II of The Mystic's Formula is to open up to a metaphysical approach. *Pretend You Already Have It* is a technique based in metaphysical understanding. In the next chapters, you will explore exactly what it means to *Pretend You Already Have It*, how to do it, and why it works.

Pretending

Remember when I said that *Pretend You Already Have It* is not a new idea? Well, here are some examples of the different ways this concept has been described and taught.

"Supply yourself with the mental equivalent, and the thing must come to you."

— Emmet Fox

"Catch the feeling of the wish fulfilled."
"Visualize *from* the end."

— Neville
metaphysical teacher

"Visualize from the heart."

— Carole Dore
PowerVision Dynamics

"Go to your virtual reality."

— Abraham-Hicks

"As a man thinketh in his heart, so is he."

— The Bible KJV

These are all different ways of saying the same thing:

> **When you pretend that you already have the thing you want, the dream you desire, you go to your imagination and pretend that it has already happened. That it is NOW your reality. That you can see it, taste it, smell it, touch it and hear it. You can feel how it would feel to have this be your experience RIGHT NOW. When you pretend you already have it, there is no longer any future. There is no longer any "some day." It is done. It has happened. It is NOW.**

Why Step 2 is Vital

The reason this step is absolutely vital to manifesting your dream is that it allows you to consciously and deliberately harness the power of the Law of Attraction. Remember, the Law of Attraction simply is. It exists. It operates in and through your life always, without exception. Just like electricity, it simply is. And just like electricity, if you don't consciously make use of it, you will miss the opportunity to benefit from its power.

At the more benign level, without electricity, you can certainly live your life, but it might be harder work and you may not get to enjoy some of the fun things electricity has to offer. It is the same with the Law of Attraction. If you do not harness its power through the conscious direction of your thoughts and emotions, your life will certainly go on, but it might be more difficult than it needs to be, and you may be missing opportunities for infinite possibility. At a more dramatic level, undirected electricity can be destructive, as a lightning bolt would demonstrate when hitting a house that lacks a grounding rod. The Law of Attraction could just as dramatically produce undesirable outcomes such as disease, poverty and hardship – all because your thoughts and emotions were allowed to *run amok* (like lightning discharging energy across the sky) without focus, direction or conscious intention. Now, this does *not* mean you can't feel your feelings. **Please understand this**. What it means is that it behooves you to have an empowering and conscious relationship with your feelings. And we'll get to that in great depth in Step III of The Formula.

The way Step II harnesses the power of the Law of Attraction is that while you're pretending you already have it, you become a magnetic *match* for the *same, i.e., for you having it!* Like attracts like. So, if in your mind's eye and in your heart of hearts, for just a moment, you really have what you want, then you'll attract that experience. And when you are focusing on lack or problems in your life, you attract more of that experience. So, when you see it, feel it and believe it in your inner world, you are essentially emitting from your sending and receiving station the vibratory frequency that you wish to receive back. In other words, you've adjusted your radio dial for the music you really want.

Yeah Buts ...

It's usually at about this time that people who are learning about these concepts start to have questions about the seeming exceptions and contradictions in the Law of Attraction and *Pretend You Already Have It.* Don't worry; we'll be addressing all of that in Step III – *Stepping Out of Your Own Way.* As I said back at the beginning, this formula is very simple but implementing and using it correctly can be a different story. Your ability to successfully use The Formula lies in understanding the deeper and subtler nuances. But before we get into all of the questions, let's make sure you really understand exactly how to do Step II.

9

How to Do It

"To refuse to recognize the creative power of man's invisible, imaginal activity is too great to be argued with. Man, through his imaginal activity, literally 'calls into existence the things that do not exist.'"

— Neville (1905-1972)
metaphysical teacher

Y ou can practice Step II of The Formula in many different ways and at any time you want. To feel most effective with it, you'll need to be in a situation where you're relatively relaxed. Commonly taught approaches to this technique include visualizing when you go to bed at night and before you arise in the morning. You can also choose a time each day to sit quietly and visualize *you living your dream* for anywhere from a few to 15 minutes a day. There are other times during the day when you can *make pretend* for a few minutes. Some of my own favorite opportunities have included:

When I'm washing the dishes in a Zen-like trance – I talk to myself, giving thanks for our wonderful housekeeper (pretend!) who keeps everything so shiny that all I have to do is rinse the occasional dish, or ...

When I'm driving my car alone – Every time I step into my car, I imagine I've passed through a magical portal into my dream life and my car is suddenly my dream car. I'm driving down the streets of Provence in France, on my way to our chateau, planning what to ask our cook to prepare for dinner, thinking about the gifts I want to send to friends back home and visualizing writing checks from one of my cash-rich accounts, or ...

When I'm in the shower – I think about the day I'm about to live, the people I'll be relating to and I see myself living my day full of joy and ease and grace, accomplishing all the things I want to accomplish, filled with patience and spontaneity, or ...

When I go to the coffee shop with my laptop computer and work on my book – I envision I already have published books circulating abundantly and this is simply my latest literary project.

It doesn't matter how you do your pretending or when you do it. You can visualize. You can talk to yourself. You can daydream. The key is for just a little while, surrender passionately to your dream, with all the love, expectancy, inspiration and receptivity you can muster. Be like a child, and let go of your adult thinking for just a few moments and transport yourself into your dream.

Living in Two Worlds

"We can go through our whole lives worrying about our future
happiness, and totally miss where true peace lives –
right here, right now."
— *Peter Russell (1946-)*
British author and film producer

It is at about this time in the learning process that people start asking questions like, "Am I supposed to live in a fantasy state all of the time?" or, "How am I supposed to live in two worlds at the same time – my reality of unpayable bills *and* the dream of financial freedom?" or, "If I'm having all these feelings of fear and stress about a certain relationship, isn't *that* vibration going to cancel out the vibration I achieve when I'm pretending all is well?"

These are very good questions and they speak to those very important subtleties I mentioned at the beginning of the book that influence greatly the degree of success you will achieve and feel in using The Formula. Let's begin delving into these subtleties with a few very important points.

We Are Multi-Dimensional Beings

"Reality is merely an illusion, albeit a very persistent one."
— *Albert Einstein*
physicist

To be a multidimensional being means there are many dimensions to us and we operate throughout multiple dimensions. This means there is much more to us than meets the eye. I realize that if you're new to this cosmic stuff, this may seem a bit far out. However, as multidimensional beings, we exist and operate in different dimensions simultaneously all the time. We just might not be aware of it. And our sensitivity to these different realms varies from person to person.

When you were offered ways to identify what you want in Step I, you were presented with different techniques and tools to help you open up to your soul's guidance. You were presented with the idea that there is a part of you, within you, that truly knows what you want and has all the answers you will ever need inside you. Well, your *soul* is also a part of you that has access to a broader perspective regarding you and your life than the *you* reacting and responding to your everyday life. This broader perspective speaks to your soul's ability, and therefore *your* ability, to tap into a broader dimension, the nonphysical dimension of energy that is the root source of all you could ever desire. So, while you're living your life with your five senses, assessing the conditions of your life, reacting to the bills you have to pay, or the body you wish were thinner, or the relationship you wish you had – there is another part of you that is *simultaneously* tapping into the very realm of energy that is consistently and constantly producing and offering back to you exactly that which you are creating with your thoughts and emotions. Keep vibrating with thoughts and feelings of *not enough money* and the Universe will keep giving you the experience of *not enough money*. Start thinking and feeling a new experience of *lots of money* and the Universe will produce and offer you *lots of money*. It is happening all the time. You may or may not be conscious of it. But once you are, and once you start to practice the conscious and deliberate directing of your thoughts and emotions, you will create on purpose rather than by default.

For the purpose of this book, we are going to be talking about two dimensions:

- *The Third Dimension* – which refers to our physical world, the realm of duality, and
- *The Dimension of the Absolute* – which refers to the realm of Source, a nonphysical realm of energy.

Those FAQs

So, in response to some of those earlier questions ...

Q: How can I coexist in both my physical reality and my visualized reality?

A: Don't worry about it. You're already doing it all the time.

Q: Am I supposed to live in a fantasy state all the time?

A: No, you do not need to live in a fantasy state all the time. As a matter of fact, all it takes is a little bit of pretending every day. This allows you to create a bridge in order for your dream to come to you from the realm of Source, which is where your dream is created. Another way of looking at it is with the radio analogy. When you pretend, you are essentially *matching* the frequency of your dream. You are tuning your receiver for the frequency you want to receive and experience.

Q: Well, what about my daily life? What if the life I'm living now is not what I want? What happens to all of those vibrations and frequencies I'm putting out that are not a match for my desire?

A: The life you have now is to be *lived!* For the sake of making your dream come true (and enjoying the life you have), the most empowering thing you can do with your present life is, as Abraham-Hicks teaches: *to make the best of it.* Make the best of what you have. Find ways to see the glass as half full. Find ways to feel good. Find things to be grateful for. The Law of Attraction will take care of the rest. When you visualize or pretend, you are always raising your vibration. And not only does high vibration attract high vibration, but it also builds strength and develops momentum. So, not only does a little go a long way, in terms of your pretending sessions being more powerful vibrationally than the vibrations of your daily life, BUT every time you find ways to feel good about the life you have, you attract to yourself more of the same – *you feeling good about the life you have.* And this ultimately produces a *life you feel good about*

High Vibrational Energy vs. Low Vibrational Energy

You know that saying, "You can catch more flies with honey than with vinegar"? This point speaks to that in the realm of vibration. High vibration is very fast and very light. High vibrational energy includes things like light and sound – things you can't hold, but you can feel or sense with your eyes and ears. Emotional energies like love, peace, joy, harmony and freedom are all high in vibration. Low frequency energy is slow and dense. The lower the vibration, the slower and denser it is. Things that are solid, that you can touch and hold with your hands, have a low vibration. Emotions like fear, anxiety, anger, and sadness, are all low in vibration.

In the honey/vinegar analogy, the idea is that, with the same amount of each, let's say one teaspoon, you can get or attract more of what you want with the sweet substance than the sour substance. The same holds true for vibration. Let's say you've been spending most of your waking hours in the low vibration of struggle, stress, anger and powerlessness regarding your job. And you start to practice for a few minutes a day imagining, pretending, visualizing and feeling what it would be like to experience total fulfillment, peace and joy in your job. The power of just a few minutes a day of the "sweet" vibration is so powerful that, gently and surely, if you raise your vibration a little everyday, you'll find yourself able to pretend with a high vibrational energy for a few more minutes each day. Like attracts like. Each feel-good thought will attract more feel-good thoughts, which attract even more feel-good thoughts until you find yourself feeling more and more positive, drawing into your experience more and more positive energy and ultimately experiencing your job more and more as you desire it. It doesn't matter that for most of your day, you struggle and feel bad. *You, by no means, have to pretend to feel good all the time in order to change your experience.* You need only start with a "teaspoon of honey" and a commitment to practice a little bit every day. Within 30 days, the momentum will take over and the high vibrational energy will be easy to access.

The Feelings Create, Not the Technique

"The feeling gets the blessing."
— *Carole Doré*
founder, PowerVision Dynamics

If you've ever watched the popular TV show *Saturday Night Live,* you may have come across a hilarious skit which featured Al Franken's character, Stuart Smalley, as the host of a show focused on self-actualization and healing. In the skit, Stuart would look at himself in a mirror reciting a long list of affirmations designed to counteract the ails of low self-esteem and self-doubt. Although this skit is very funny, it really captures a common perception that techniques such as affirmations and visualizations are ridiculous, ineffective and laughable – not to be taken at all seriously.

The reason these metaphysical techniques have gotten a bad rap is only because they have been misunderstood and misinterpreted. Many people have incorrectly believed that the power of these techniques lies in form and frequency. These techniques have been approached with an emphasis on controlling the mind. In other words, people have believed that if they say the affirmations enough, or visualize the right image enough, they will be successful in their goal. This is only partly true. To approach these techniques in a mechanical way will produce limited results, at best. Worse yet is when people think "more is better" and approach these tools like homework, emphasizing steadfast commitment and repetition.

Let me tell you right now: *If you aren't having fun with this stuff, it won't work very well.* Your true power as a creative being lies in your emotional energy. The true power in any or all of these techniques lies in the emotional energy *behind* the words or visualizations. The truth is, if you did nothing more than find ways to feel good more of the time, you'd start to magnetize your dream to you with more and more power and speed.

To put thoughts and emotions in perspective, think of it this way: Your positive emotional energy is the force that brings your dreams to life. Your thoughts give form and focus to the energy. For example, your thoughts may give form and focus to an idea – let's say a toaster. Without the electrical energy to bring it to life, the toaster is just going to sit there taking up space but not very useful, not very helpful and not very fulfilling. The same is true with affirmations and visualization. The affirmation, "I love myself" is a nice idea, but if you have no positive emotional energy to bring it to life, you can repeat the affirmation until you are blue in the face, but your capacity to love yourself more than before will not likely expand much.

The feeling gets the blessing means that whatever the true emotional energy is underlying any thoughts, words or actions, that's the vibration the Universe will match. If you tell yourself, "I love myself," but underneath the words, you feel like a piece of dirt, you will attract more of you *feeling like a piece of dirt.* For this reason, it's vitally important that you develop an honest relationship with your emotions. (Don't worry. There's a whole chapter dedicated to this in Step III of The Formula.) And if you want to be successful with this, make sure that above all else, you make *feeling good and having fun* much more important than technique.

Progress Not Perfection

One of the biggest misconceptions people fall prey to is the feeling that: "You have to do this perfectly if you're going to change your reality." People think they can't feel bad or think any negative thoughts or they will "counter-create," i.e., cancel out what they are trying to draw into their experience. This is simply not true and if you fall prey to this type of thinking, it will sabotage your efforts more than if you just let yourself feel bad when you do. Here is the classic ERRONEOUS line of thinking:

"Okay, I know what I want and I need to focus on what I want, pretending I already have it and feeling the feeling of the wish fulfilled. I want to create financial freedom and I've been visualizing, but I've got $10,000 in unpaid bills, and don't know how I'm going to pay them. I'm totally stressed out but I can't think about that or I'll counter-create. I need to relax and feel good, but no matter what I do, I can't. I keep obsessing about these bills. Okay, just say your affirmations. Okay, that's not helping. I'm still stressed, but I just can't go there ..." and the gerbil wheel spins and spins and spins.

What happens is that these thoughts and feelings start circling in your head. You may feel obsessed – fabricating and running different scenarios in your mind. Maybe you'll yell at your kids, or get a headache or isolate yourself. And you'll stay in this place for a *long time*. No matter what you do, you can't shift into a high vibration. You can't connect with your dream. Why? *Because you're afraid to think or feel thoughts that are contrary to your desire*. The problem is that in an attempt to *control* your thoughts and feelings you are creating *resistance*. Resistance and low vibrational energy essentially present the same conditions – they limit your ability to be a vibrational match to your desire.

When the conditions of your life are stressing you out, activating fear and doubt, find ways to honor your feelings so that they can come up, come out and release. Once they release, you will feel relief and an opening for feeling better will reveal itself. When you judge or resist your feelings, or try to talk yourself out of them, you are resisting them. Resistance blocks the flow of well-being which is your nature, and the high vibrational energy that magnetizes your desire to you.

More on Resistance

So you might better understand how this all works, let's recap some fundamental principles, as they were addressed in Chapter 5 – Metaphysics 101:

There is only One and that One is God or Source Energy. Be-cause the nature of Source Energy is infinite and all-good, the natural expression of it is unconditional love, perfect health, lim-itless wealth and success, fulfillment in every way, and all that is good. And because there is only One energy that expresses in, as, and through All That Is, then you must, by definition, be made up of this same energy. You are an individualized expres-sion of this infinite well-being.

This means your natural state – your essence, who you *real-ly* are – is *all of this*. You embody these same qualities, and your natural state is well-being. It follows then, that if this is your natural state, feeling bad is *unnatural* to you. So, you may ask, "If it is unnatural to feel bad in any way, then why do I feel bad? The answer: **resistance**.

When you think thoughts that are contrary to your soul's inner knowing, your infinite and divine nature, your soul, sends you "feel-bad" feelings to tell you that you are presenting block-ages or obstructions to the flow of your well-being. When you honor your emotions, you are allowing them to serve their pur-pose, which is to inform you that you're thinking thoughts that will limit your ability to create that which you desire. When you try to *talk yourself out of feeling bad, or force yourself to feel good when you just can't,* then you are resisting your emo-tions and preventing them from guiding you back to your soul's truth.

Sometimes you can simply shift your attention toward what you want and thoughts that feel better. Other times, you cannot and need to gradually move toward feeling better by honoring your feelings and experiencing greater and greater relief as you move toward feeling better.

It is when people mistakenly think they are supposed to "do this feel-good pretending thing" perfectly and deny their emo-tional navigational system that they create the very resistance they are trying to avoid for fear that feeling bad will cancel out their manifestations. However, Abraham-Hicks teaches us that *we manifest that which is the balance of our thoughts.*

In other words, when you look at a certain topic in your life and blend together all the thoughts and emotions you hold on that topic, your manifested experience will be an out-picturing of all those vibrations melded together. Let's look at the topic of money. Let's say that sometimes you think money is great. Sometimes, you think you can't be spiritual and make good money. Sometimes, you focus a lot of attention on your debt. Sometimes, you vibrate enthusiasm for a lucrative idea. Sometimes, you can be grateful for what you have. Sometimes, you fret about not having enough. Take *all* of these vibrations, put them in a bowl, mix them up, and your manifested experience will be the result – the balance of your vibration.

Another simplified way that I like to look at it is this way: If you think and feel abundance 49% of the time and think and feel scarcity 51% of the time, the balance of this is 2% more scarcity, so scarcity is what you manifest. If you can match the vibration of abundance just 2% more of the time, you've shifted the balance over to abundance and that begins to show up in your life. **So, you see, you don't have to direct your thoughts and emotions perfectly, 100% of the time. You need only move in the right direction. Progress, not perfection, will keep your dreams moving toward you.**

10

Variations on the Same Theme

Although *Pretending You Already Have It* is the title name for Step II, it is not all inclusive of other techniques that accomplish the same objective. The objective of Step II is to become a vibrational match to that which you desire so that through the Law of Attraction, you can draw your desire to you. Another title for Step II could have been *BE What You Want*, but I thought that would be a bit more challenging to grasp. So, I framed Step II around pretending, knowing that it could serve as a spring board to other techniques that allow you to achieve that ever-so-important vibrational match. What follows here are some other techniques that are just as powerful as pretending, visualizing, and imagining. As with Step I, where numerous techniques are offered for identifying what you want, all of these techniques work and you get to use them and play with them in whatever way feels best. You can use one, some, or all of these techniques. All are effective and powerful.

Gratitude

"Make me sweet again, fragrant and fresh and wild,
And thankful for any small event."
— *Rumi (1207-1223)*
Muslim Persian poet, theologian, teacher of Sufism

Having an "attitude of gratitude" is another one of those expressions that is highly underrated and often misunderstood to be nothing more than nicey-nice fluff. Gratitude is a profoundly powerful state of consciousness and a tool for a fulfilling life and for the manifestation of your dreams. Gratitude is the most powerful prayer you can think or utter, for it is a declaration of *having*. When you acknowledge and feel that you *have*, you attract more *having*. So, when you have nothing more than $17.32 to your name, you can either focus on all the money you lack and all that you can *not* afford to buy, or you can give thanks for this blessing of money and all the food you can buy, or that you have enough to give two dollars to someone who has even less than you.

Practicing an attitude of gratitude is the practice of counting your blessings. It is the discipline of looking to what you do have versus at what you *don't* have, and giving thanks – heartfelt thanks – for it. It is about looking for the good, no matter how bad things look. This practice alone has the power to turn your life around for the better, no matter what the conditions are, no matter how much evidence you have to build a case about how bad things are. When you build a case, you focus on the bad … and you attract more of the unwanted. When you focus on the good, you attract that.

Amy, the 17-year-old daughter of one of my dearest friends, was diagnosed with a rare and aggressive form of cancer at the age of 16, right in the midst of an otherwise joyous time in this family's life. Scholarly honors, driver's licenses, proms, graduations and celebrations made up their world at the time. The cancer had already spread to her lungs, and the doctors gave the family some statistics that would have brought anyone to their knees. Once they found their breath again after the initial shock, the family embarked on a journey to support Amy through what was to be a grueling year of aggressive cancer treatments. As an intimate witness to this journey, I saw the mother and the daughter draw upon the power of gratitude during one of the most challenging times of their lives. The mother would ask her daughter every day, "What is one thing you can be grateful for?" One day, the answer was, "My toe doesn't hurt."

In a long car-ride conversation with Amy after she had survived not only the cancer treatments, but the cancer itself, I asked her, "How did you do it?" And among the many wisdoms she shared with me, I remember a particular example of the power of gratitude. Her cancer had been causing extreme pain in her foot and she said, "When my foot would hurt, I would give thanks that I could feel the pain in my foot because it meant I still *had* a foot." I learned then that amputation had been a possibility discussed in previous medical consultations.

There is never a shortage of evidence to build cases for how hard our lives are or can be at times. Amy and her mother had plenty of opportunity and valid reason to turn their attention toward their struggle, the unfairness of it all, the pain, the stress, the terror and the financial hardship. They knew, however, they did not have the luxury of indulging in negativity. Of course, they felt their feelings. Of course, fear, stress, fatigue, anger and confusion were regular companions during their journey But, rather than pitching a tent in "the valley of the shadow of death," they walked on through, always looking for the good of Divine Spirit to be revealed. They would **meet** their emotions with respect, honor them through acknowledgment and keep looking for the good.

At the time of this writing, Amy is celebrating seven years free and clear of cancer. She is considered a miracle by western medical standards. And, although I can offer no formula that guarantees the survival of a life-threatening illness, I can tell you this: The power of gratitude, the power of connecting to the good of Source, the power of seeing and feeling yourself as well – no matter what your body is doing, no matter what the doctors are saying – is the substance miracles are made of. Miracles *do* happen everyday and they are not beyond your control. You have the power to create miracles in your life by tapping into your power as a co-creative being with the Universe.

There are various ways to be in gratitude. Some teachers encourage you to keep a gratitude journal and, every night when you go to bed, write down five things for which you are grateful. Others speak of having an attitude of gratitude, which is to always seek that for which you can be grateful. My greatest discipline is to give thanks when something does *not* go my way. And one of the greatest practices is to give thanks for the blessings you can *not* see. When you are experiencing a situation you do not want, if you remember there is only one source for all that is, and that Source is all-good, then you must understand that there is good in that situation, even if you do not see it. **The trick is to suspend judgment.** If you judge something as bad, you have focused your thoughts and emotions in such a way that you *must*, by the Law of Attraction, experience it as bad. When you judge something as bad, you erect walls that prevent the good from being revealed to you. A powerful way to be in gratitude when something undesired occurs is to practice the following mantra:

It is what it is.
Source is always good.
There is good here and I give thanks for it,
even if I can not see it.
I am open and receptive to experiencing the good.

Affirmative Prayer

Affirmative prayer builds upon the power of gratitude, the power of acknowledging that God (or Source or Spirit or whatever) is *always good*, and the power of recognizing that you, as an individualized expression of this one source, embody the same omni-beneficent qualities. The reason affirmative prayer works is that it guides your conscious mind through a step-by-step process that is based in logical understanding. As you consciously connect with logical, positive truth, your emotional state shifts into a vibrational match with what you desire. Remember, words are not enough to achieve a vibrational match. Your emotions must be in alignment as well.

For this reason, affirmative prayer is very powerful because it requires the person praying to go beyond words. If you are not connecting with the prayer on an emotional level, you are not doing it correctly. And in comparison to some forms of prayer that are stated as requests, affirmative prayer is formed as a series of acknowledgments, or declarations, such as: "I already have this. It is so. It is here. It is now. It is done."

There are five steps in affirmative prayer, as taught in New Thought theology. You do not have to follow this particular order, although I've discovered that when you're trying to get your logical mind and emotional state to align in a positive direction, this particular order builds upon itself in a very powerful way.

1. Recognition
2. Unification
3. Realization
4. Thanksgiving
5. Release

Here's another way to look at the five steps of affirmative prayer:

1. God Is
2. I AM
3. The Truth (of the situation) Is _____
4. Gratitude
5. Let Go and Let God

It is a good idea to begin your prayer by taking some deep breaths, relaxing and turning your attention within. The act of turning your attention within is one of creating a space for you to connect with your soul – that broader aspect of you connected to Source. Once you have shifted your attention from the outside world toward your internal world, you begin by making statements about what **God Is.** Some examples could include:

> "I know there is only One. One Power. One Presence. One Life. And I know that this power, this presence, is God and it expresses in, as, and through me. I know that God is Divine Love and All Goodness. And so, I know that God is infinite well-being, perfect health, infinite abundance and prosperity, harmony, peace, joy and freedom. I also know that God is all powerful and so there is nothing beyond God's reach. There is nothing that God cannot make new again."

The idea is to keep making statements *you believe* until you can feel yourself connecting with the infinite well-being of Source (or the infinite power of God's love and grace). Once you are *feeling* that shift beginning to happen, then you move into Step 2 – I AM. Your I AM statements are based in the logical understanding that you are made up of the same substance as Source and therefore possess the very same qualities you were just talking about in Step 1. Some examples could include:

> "I also know that I AM an individualized expression of this same energy. Because there is only One, I must, by definition be a part of this One. And so I know I possess all of the same qualities as this Source Energy. I realize that the TRUTH of who I am is this. And so I fully understand I AM infinite well-being, perfect health, infinite abundance and prosperity, harmony, peace, joy and freedom. This is my true essence."

Once you begin connecting with the infinite potential of who you really are, then you can move into making declarative statements about the truth of the situation you wish to transform. If, for example, you are struggling in your marriage and your dream is to experience joy, freedom, love and ease, you could make statements such as:

> "I know the truth of my marriage is that Divine Spirit is present within it because God is everywhere present. Spirit expresses in, as, and through me, my husband, my marriage – all of life. And because Divine Spirit is love, peace, harmony, joy, ease and grace, I know that somewhere in my marriage, these qualities exist. I also know that if I suspend judgment, I remain open to experiencing all the good that is present in my relationship. And so, I allow the infinite power of the Divine to express freely in my relationship, right here, right now."

Once you have really felt the truth and infinite potential of the situation at hand, then you can move into gratitude, which is about giving thanks for the fact that what you desire already exists. It is already so. It is already done. Although you may not see it, by the time you've reached this point in your affirmative prayer, you should be able to feel that the *truth* of what you desire already exists energetically, because that is the nature of the Universe. Everything that is, has ever been, or will ever be, already exists energetically. All you need to do is to align yourself with it so you may allow it into your experience. Remember, gratitude is one of the most powerful vibrations you can emit because it is the consciousness of *having*. Examples of gratitude statements could include:

> "I give grateful thanks for the grace and ease that bless my marriage always. I give thanks for the love I have known in my relationship and for my willingness to experience greater love and possibility. I thank Spirit for guiding me to my highest and greatest good and for my ability to let go and trust that the highest good is working through my relationship right now."

The final step of affirmative prayer is release. This speaks to releasing all of the details to the Universe, understanding that there is nothing left for you to do now. The Universe has already provided for your desire. You have already achieved a vibrational match through reconnecting to the truth of the Universe, yourself and your situation. And now, the Law of Attraction does the rest. Examples of statements of release can include:

> "I now willingly release this entire situation (relationship, person, condition) unto the Law, knowing full well that, before even asking, it is given. I allow the infinite power of the Universe to harmonize and adjust every aspect of my life in the perfect way and for the highest and greatest good. And so it is. Amen."

So, this is how you do affirmative prayer. At first, you may want to lean on the formula. But as you practice, you will notice it becomes easier and more free-flowing. It's almost as if the prayer takes on a life of its own, because what happens is, you discover that through the process, you open up to Source Energy moving through you with greater ease. You may even notice that the focus and content of your prayer become secondary to the powerful experience of connecting with Source. And when you connect with Source, you'll notice your vibration becomes higher and that you're able to maintain a higher vibration more often and for longer periods of time.

Acting As If (i.e., Acting on Faith)

> "I pretended to be somebody I wanted to be until
> I finally became that person.
> Or he became me."
> — *Cary Grant (1904 – 1986)*
> *English-born, American movie star*

Acting As If is another powerful variation of pretending. To *act as if* is to act as if you already have your dream. In other words, you take the actions you would take if your desire were already granted or guaranteed. For example, let's say you want to buy a new car but don't have the money at the moment. Rather than stay at home worrying about not having the money, or lamenting that you can't have a new car because you don't know where the money would come from, you *act as if* getting your new car is a guaranteed event. So, you would do things like research the cars you like on the Internet. Go to dealerships and test drive your favorite cars. Fill out loan applications without a care in the world. Get the idea?

To *act is if* is to act on faith. Ah ... *faith*. That one word can suddenly change the feeling of this whole technique. If you already have a strong concept of faith, then to act on faith may be an extension of something that feels natural to you. If, however, faith feels like some intangible, magical thinking, this technique may challenge you. I'm not asking you to summon blind faith, which lends itself to believing in something just because I say so. Instead, I'm asking you to put your faith in your growing understanding of how the Universe works. If everything I've said so far in this book is too *airy fairy* for you, then start getting concrete. Look to the hard factual world of science. Again, I refer you to the Recommended Resources section in the Appendix. Everyday, more and more scientific research emerges that supports the idea that there is an energetic universe, and that it's malleable to our thoughts, emotions and actions. To *act as if* and to *act on faith* is to act upon a deeper understanding of how the Universe works that lies beyond your five senses.

Find Your Role Models

"If you want to be successful, find someone who has achieved the results you want and copy what they do ... and you'll achieve the same results."

— Tony Robbins (1960 -)
internationally renowned success coach

One of the easiest and most effective ways to practice *Acting As If* is to find role models and do what they do. In other words, whoever you may want to be, whatever you want to accomplish, find someone who is doing it or has done it and become a copycat.

In my late 20s, I was accepted into graduate school, which was a huge dream come true. But as it happened, the timing seemed less than ideal. My life was filled with several other time-consuming commitments – I had a full-time paying job I loved; I was commuting four hours a day; I had a full-time volunteer job; I attended meetings several nights a week; and I was in a successful romantic relationship with my boyfriend (now my husband). When I got the letter of acceptance to graduate school, I was both thrilled and overwhelmed. *How on earth am I going to do it all?* I simply did *not* want to give up anything I had going on in my life. And I didn't even know how I was going to afford school, let alone manage it all. And so, in addition to *Acting As If,* where I kept placing one foot in front of the other as if graduating with my masters degree was a done deal, I looked for and found my role model, and assumed her identity.

Gwen was my inspiration and she was doing it all! Gwen was one of the most successful women I knew. She had a full-time job as the director of a nonprofit, she volunteered in high leadership capacities, she went to graduate school, and she maintained her relationships with love and care. I thought, "If Gwen can do it, it's possible." And with each and every challenge I encountered, I asked myself, "What would Gwen do?" Then I'd do it. And if I didn't know, I'd ask her.

When there weren't enough hours in a day and I was living on little sleep, I'd ask: "What would Gwen do?" When I'd moved mountains to have just one day with my boyfriend and a mandatory emergency meeting was called on that same day, I'd ask, "What would Gwen do?" When I had twenty phone calls to return, three papers to write, and my boss was pushing a big deadline, "What would Gwen do?" And so it was, for 5½ years of not knowing how I could possibly succeed, I'd do what I thought Gwen would do, and I graduated. And, if that wasn't enough, I got married, we bought our first home, and I rose to the rank of regional coordinator for the nonprofit I loved. By doing what Gwen would do, I experienced success, as she had.

Finding your role models and doing what they would do is a fun and easy way to harness the power of pretending. Just as with all aspects of Step II of The Formula, you never need to know *how* it will happen; you simply need to know and focus on *what you want.*

Give, Serve, Offer

"The only ones among you who will be really happy
are those who will have sought and found how to serve."
— *Albert Schweitzer (1875-1965)*
German theologian, philosopher and physician

I was truly awakened to the abundance-generating power of giving, serving and offering in my late 20s when I had joined a nonprofit organization that was heavily dependent on volunteers for its operations. Up until that time, I had been pretty self-focused. I had gone through my adolescence like the average American kid singing the tune, "It's all about me!" Then after college, I embarked on even more self-focused activities such as therapy, self-help books, journaling and personal growth workshops. All of my energy and consciousness were focused on *getting*. How could I *get* more understanding? How could I *get* a boyfriend? How could I *get* a good job? How could I *get* happiness? I'd ask these questions. I'd take action. And I'd *get* many of these things – all except for the happiness part.

Then one day, I joined a volunteer-run organization and learned about a concept that was new to me: *being of service.* Being of service meant to give for the sake of giving. Openhearted. No strings attached. No expectation of *getting* anything back. Being of service was about getting the focus off of me and putting it on others. Being of service was about giving not getting. Being of service was about putting 100% of my attention on offering my energy out, for the benefit of others, rather than trying to pull energy in for my own benefit. Now *this* was a truly novel idea to me!

As I started volunteering, I encountered some painful, embarrassing and yet gorgeously life-changing experiences. I learned that I operated from survival mode – that my basic consciousness was one of lack. I believed there was never enough money, love or attention to go round. I discovered that my basic mind-set was one of separation. Because I felt separate from Source, I felt alone, abandoned or unsupported by people, life and God. Consequently, my *modus operandi* was to fend for myself. Life *was* about getting or taking faster than the other guy. I didn't feel safe, and believed I had to watch out for myself.

When you see the world as a place to survive, the act of giving can be very challenging. It requires a huge shift in consciousness. You must leap the chasm from not-enoughness to believing you *are* enough, that you have plenty to give, that there will always be more, that you will be taken care of, that you are safe and loved, and that life is to be lived, not just survived. And, as it happened for me, if you dare to leap this chasm, you may find yourself bumping up against your limiting human tendencies, instincts and states of consciousness (more on that in Step III).

However, here's the thing: When I started giving – *really* giving with no strings attached, with my focus on others and not myself, with no expectation of getting – something miraculous happened. It was like the Grinch whose heart grew ten sizes that day. All of a sudden, where before I couldn't *get* enough to get happy, I was overflowing with love and fulfillment. I was experiencing the joy of making a difference in other people's lives. I was experiencing true connection with other souls. I was experiencing a love I had never known – an expansive, life-changing spiritual love for others. Essentially, Source Energy was flowing through me. I was doing more than I had ever done, but sleeping less and had lots of physical energy to spare.

People who knew my life would ask, "How do you do it all?" And the answer, as corny as it sounds, was "Love." Love was my fuel. Love – that expansive, high-vibrational energy – was harmonizing and adjusting all the details in my life so that everything would work. This was the same chapter in my life when I practiced the technique of *What would Gwen Do?* Oh sure, there were times I was overwhelmed, or I'd make big mistakes. But I learned that you can have a life where you are screwing up all over the place in the little things, but in the big scheme of things, you're living a magnificently successful life.

The two keys to success were: 1) maintaining a consciousness of giving, and 2) doing things in my life that I really wanted to be doing. The only times I felt overwhelmed, resentful or tired was when I either forgot the miracle of giving, or I let myself become a victim to the choices I had made in my life. When, for example, I found myself resenting my job because, "I'm overworked, underpaid, and it just isn't as much fun as my volunteer work," then I'd suddenly get very tired. So, in those moments, I would say to myself, "Okay, if your job is so horrible, then get another one. No one is making you stay here. You're not a victim." This would lead me to remember I had choices. And this would in turn lead me to really explore whether I wanted to keep my job or leave. Once I started weighing the pros and cons, I'd eventually see the gifts my job had to offer and remember I was actually grateful for my job and was *choosing* to stay (as opposed to having no choice).

So, why is *being of service* so powerful? From a manifestation perspective, when you give what you have, you are telling the Universe vibrationally, "I have this. As a matter of fact, I have so much of it that I have extra to spare." So, what does the Universe do with this? It matches your vibration and gives you more of what you are saying, thinking, feeling and demonstrating that you have.

When you give love freely, love comes back to you multiplied. When you circulate money, *freely and with gratitude,* money comes back to you multiplied. When you give time and support, the Universe provides evermore. The key to this, again, is your *underlying feeling* when you give, serve or offer. If you can *not* give from a place of faith, love, freedom, gratitude and generosity, don't do it. Remember, the *feeling* creates, not the *technique.*

Affirmations You Actually Buy In To

"In the beginning was the Word, and the Word was with God,
and the Word was God."
— *John 1:1, Holy Bible, KJV*

Affirmations are positive statements designed to focus your attention toward that which you want. Affirmations can be spoken or written. I highly recommend writing your affirmations down and posting them someplace you'll see them regularly. You can say them as many times a day as you like. They are reminders of *positive truths* you feed your mind and heart when you need an extra vibrational lift, or when:

- You find your consciousness wavering towards what you *don't want,* or
- You are reacting to the conditions of your life, such as feeling kind of low, or
- Your brain goes on overdrive (as it can tend to do) fixating, obsessing or fabricating all sorts of negative scenarios.

Affirmations can be used as part of your daily practice to stay focused on what you want, starting and ending each day with heartfelt declarations that move you towards your desire. They can also be used as a management tool, when your thoughts and emotions are taking you *away* from what you're trying to create. However you use affirmations, there is one fundamental aspect that determines their usefulness: **You must choose positive statements you truly believe.**

Remember how I mentioned that affirmations have gotten a bad rap? Well, that's because they have been misunderstood and used incorrectly. Done right, however, affirmations can and do work. But if they are to work, you must really *believe* what you're saying and you must say them with lots of positive feeling.

Affirmations do *not* work when you're trying to convince yourself of something you just don't buy. The reason for this is that *feelings* create, not technique. And it is your *vibration* that the Universe matches, not the words. So if your words say, "I'm beautiful just the way I am," but your underlying feelings *vibrate,* "I'm fat and I don't like my body," you will attract more thoughts and experiences of fatness and you not liking your body.

Sometimes positive affirmations are easy to create. You simply find something positive you know to be true, and focus on it. When this is the case, you can repeat the affirmations often and they easily help you feel lighter and more positive about your desire and the direction in which you are moving. Other times, it's more difficult to find something positive to focus on about a given situation. You may feel stuck in old emotions or beliefs that make it feel impossible to shift the way you think about something. If this is the case, two highly effective ways for creating affirmations are:

- **Statements of Willingness** – where you build your affirmation around what you *are* willing to learn, discover or experience; and
- **If/Then Statements** – where you make your mind focus on possibility by identifying evidence and logical truths that support where you want to go.

For example, if you want to love and accept yourself but deep down you know you don't, saying an affirmation such as: "I love and accept myself exactly the way I am," simply won't work. However, if you know you're *willing to learn* how to love and accept yourself exactly as you are, an affirmation such as, "I'm *willing* to learn how to love and accept myself completely," would be very powerful.

If, for example, you want to experience abundance and prosperity in your life, but no matter where you turn, all you can see and feel is scarcity, then an affirmation such as, "I am a financially free multimillionaire," will be ineffective. But, if you have a role model who went from rags to riches and who you can truly relate to, an affirmation such as, "**If** Zena McMurphy can so dramatically transform her life to one of such freedom and wealth, **then** I can, too," could really shift your energy toward what you are creating. The key to creating and using affirmations is that you must find a statement which you resonate with completely. That is, it has to be something you believe and know to be true for you.

There are times, though, that no matter how hard you try, you just can't find a positive truth on which to focus. You just don't believe your dream is possible in any way, shape or form. Or you may have come to realize you're really *not willing* to do the work, make the shift, or allow yourself the possibility. In this situation, you have some limiting beliefs that need deeper work. For this level of exploration, refer to *Limiting Beliefs* in Step III.

Finding a Familiar Frame of Reference

Becoming a vibrational match for what you desire is the name of the game, agreed? Well, what if you can't even *imagine* what it would *feel* like to be, have or do what you dream of? What if your dream is to have a successful relationship but you just can't imagine what that would look or feel like? Maybe you come from a family broken by divorce. Maybe you're surrounded by friends who are soured by their history of failed relationships. Maybe you have never really had a fulfilling experience in relationships.

What if you dream of being debt-free and financially free, but have been carrying debt for as long as you can remember? What if, even in your most passionate attempts to *pretend with commitment*, you just can't seem to *catch the feeling*?

Finding a familiar frame of reference is a very powerful tool to help you in these circumstances. And it just so happens that both of the aforementioned scenarios are not hypothetical. They were my experience and what follows are examples of how to become a vibrational match for something you really struggle to imagine.

The Unreachable Dream

By the time I was in my late 20s, I'd had my fair share of failure in the realm of relationships. I'd been in therapy for several years and had become quite involved in personal growth work focused on learning how to create successful relationships between men and women. My history with men included fearing them, avoiding them, dating them once or twice and never seeing them again, falling in "obsession" with men who were unavailable (emotionally, geographically or otherwise) and feeling lonely, hopeless, desperate and like a loser. I feared that it could never happen for me. I watched women who seemed effortlessly comfortable around men, and here I was, walking down the street, avoiding eye-contact with men. I was considered quite attractive in my time and had a lot to offer in every way but I was so lost as to how to just BE myself, let alone like or love myself, that it didn't matter how good the package was. My internal vibration of: "I am unlovable, unworthy and afraid" drew to me the experience of unlovable, unworthy and afraid.

There was no way I could have ever *faked it 'til I made it*, because I couldn't even touch what it might be to feel successful in a relationship. That is until one day, a friend and coach helped me find a familiar frame of reference. All of a sudden, I could connect with how it would *feel* to have a successful relationship with a man. I had been setting goals about relationships with men, but the "big dream," the "whole shebang," THE Relationship was too much of a leap for me, given where I was. My friend guided me to start smaller. She said, "You're never going to have a successful relationship with a man until you feel safe with men and feel you can trust them. Let's start there. Who is one man you feel safe with? One man you trust?" I racked my brain. There was NO ONE. Not a single one. And then she asked, "What about your brother?" Pause ... "Ohhhhhh, my brother! Yes, of course. Yes. I do feel safe with him. And I totally trust him."

She guided me in further goal-setting and some homework assignments, but the gist of it all was that she helped me *catch the feeling* of a successful relationship with a man. And from that point on, I would focus on that success, that feeling. I didn't realize it at the time but I was matching the vibration every time I thought of my relationship with my brother. I was visualizing having this experience of safety and trust with other men and every time, I would think of my brother because a deep part of me knew that if it was possible with him, it was possible with other men.

Acknowledging Your Successes

Another variation on the theme of matching the vibration of your dream fulfilled has to do with the *long-term attitude* you maintain while moving towards your dreams. Let's face it, instant manifestation of a dream is great fun but what if your dream is a long time coming and takes years to manifest? How do you keep your vibration up and positive?

There are simply dreams that take a long time to manifest. There are many reasons for this:

- Maybe you have some healing or growing to do before your consciousness is at a place to match your dream.
- Maybe your dream hasn't manifested because the Universe is orchestrating details for your highest good in a way you cannot possibly understand.
- Maybe you're still in Step I of The Formula, clarifying what you want.
- Maybe you don't know why.

Regardless of the reason, your dream might be slow in coming. I've seen this scenario countless times in my own life and in the lives of others. There is a common pitfall that can push your dream away ... and an easy solution to keep it coming toward you. Whether your dream is to heal your body from a dire health diagnosis, manifest the relationship of your dreams or become financially free, if your dream has not manifested over the long haul, it's not uncommon to feel discouraged, to lose hope and to even feel depressed sometimes. **The mistake people make here (this is the pitfall) is to believe that because it hasn't happened yet, it won't happen at all.**

So here you've been steadily drawing in your dream but you are going through an unusually difficult time. Maybe you've felt particularly ill lately, or a woman hasn't accepted a date with you in eight months, or you're still in debt after ten years. When you feel particularly hopeless or discouraged, this is the time to take stock of your successes. Often times, we are so intently focused on the end result that if that exact result hasn't manifested, we think nothing is happening. But when you stop and take a look, you will see you *are* making progress. And it's in noticing your progress, and acknowledging the small successes along the way, that you'll be able to keep going and keep your vibration up. **Your goal is to be able to recognize and declare, "It's really happening! Maybe slowly but I'm doing it!"**

Laurie was a friend and a client who was literally a 40-year-old virgin. She, like most of us, wanted a successful, romantic relationship. And God bless her, she was willing to do the work. She did therapy, she did personal growth workshops, she read books, she took risks, she wrote visions, she enlisted the support of girlfriends – she did it all! And year after year, as she held her dream in front of her, her relationship was nowhere to be seen. Believe me, Laurie lost hope at times. It was painful to see someone work so hard and still, no relationship. But with the help of friends, she kept her eye on the prize. Sometimes she'd break down crying, unable to hold her dream for herself. So, her friends would tell her they'd hold her dream for her. Sometimes she had to allow herself to wonder: "What if this really isn't going to happen for me?" and let go of control for the hundredth time. Yet, whenever she'd hit the wall, thinking, "Nothing's happening, I work so hard, but nothing's happening," her friends would remind her, "But Laurie, look how far you've come! Two years ago, you'd never even been on a date and now you've started dating! And this year, you've been kissing! Remember how insecure you used to be? Now look at how flirty and confident you've become." By focusing on her little successes along the way, Laurie kept her vibration up and kept moving forward. Today, she is a happily married woman.

And then there was Alex, a man who wanted to create financial freedom. However, debt seemed to be his primary demon. He had begun his relationship with debt in college when he got snagged by the credit card companies and had been in debt ever since. Now, at age 37, he was still in debt. He watched financial advisors on TV, read books, made commitments to himself to live below his means, and pay off his debt once and for all. He studied metaphysics and worked on his prosperity consciousness. He'd do well with his commitment for a while, but would fall off the wagon and pull out his credit cards again.

Then one day, he watched yet another show that turned him on to yet another book, and he made yet another commitment to be debt-free and set-free. This time he cut up his cards. He had realized that as long as he kept his credit cards "for emergencies," he was never *really* going to allow Source to be his source of financial supply. He realized he was making his credit cards his source. Now armed with a renewed sense of commitment and the wisdom that came from many years of seeming failure and much metaphysical study, he tried again. He owed over $100,000 – a combination of business and personal debt. So, for two years, he lived on cash only and he lived below his means, making sacrifices and sending every extra cent he had toward his debt.

During a particularly discouraging time, he found himself thinking about how, after all these years, he was *still in debt!* He was feeling down and discouraged, when suddenly his soul spoke to him, "Hey, buddy! Yes, you're still in debt, but you only owe $55,000! You're really doing it! It's happening. You may not be debt free yet but it IS happening!" With the encouragement of this still, small voice in his head, Alex was able to see that his dream *really was coming true*. He acknowledged his successes. And from that day forward, whenever his attention wandered over to his debt, he would look only at how much he had paid off. Although, Alex is still paying off his debt today, he now knows without a shadow of a doubt that this dream is a done deal! And he now easily allows his vibration to match the feeling of the wish fulfilled.

Living Step II of The Formula

Pretending You Have It requires you to draw upon some mystical qualities in the way you live your daily life. Integrating this step essentially requires you to live in two dimensions – your third-dimensional reality, which is no more than an *effect* of your consciousness, and your inner reality, which is the *cause* of what you experience. This can be quite a leap for some. This way of seeing life and your world is the road less traveled and yet it is THE road to fulfillment.

It's really not as hard as it may sound and can be a lot of fun. Your opportunity is to see what life is giving you and remember: *This is not real.* If you like what you're seeing, enjoy it, give thanks and reap the benefits of your high vibration. If you don't like what you're seeing, do as Carole Dore of PowerVision Dynamics teaches us: "Thumb your nose at the third dimension and then focus on what you want." You now have an arsenal of techniques to keep your attention focused on what you want with positive energy. The more you do this, the more natural and easy it will become to live in both dimensions. And as your vibration draws to you more of what you want, your outer experience and your inner consciousness will become more aligned, gently erasing the source of seeming conflicts.

As you move on to Step III of The Formula, you'll learn exactly how to step out of your own way, when the inevitable challenges of living in two dimensions arise. Onward!

THE MYSTIC'S FORMULA
Step III:

Step Out of Your Own Way

11

Letting Go,
Being Open,
Being Receptive

"The world is ruled by letting things take their course.
It cannot be ruled by interfering."
— *Lao Tsu (6th century BCE)*
founder of Taoism

To step out of your own way is to understand there is a force in the Universe greater than you that can make all of your dreams come true if you let it. To step out of your own way is to surrender, over and over again, to the idea that this source is All-Good, All-Powerful, All-Loving and All-Knowing. To step out of your own way is to accept that the scope of *your* power in your life, in comparison to the power of Source in your life, is analogous to the power a child has over his life in comparison to that of his or her parent. *(And, much like children, we think we know it all and resist our parents when they try to do what they know is best for us in the bigger scheme of things.)* To step out of your own way is to practice the discipline of refraining from judging something you don't like as *bad*, so as to stay open to the inevitable good that *must*, by definition of Source, be present in every situation and condition. To step out of your own way is to do *your* job and let the Universe do *its* job.

Stepping out of your own way is a state of consciousness, a way of *being*. It is not something you *do*. And because it is not something you do, because it is not something you can engage in with your five senses, it requires faith. The more you feed your faith with *understanding*, the easier it is to access your faith. And the stronger your faith, the more peace, joy, love, freedom and gratitude you experience in your journey towards success. The less understanding you have of the laws of the Universe, the more your faith feels blind and therefore scarier and more difficult to access. This chapter is dedicated to helping you understand further the laws of the Universe, so that you may allow this force to empower you as you create your life with greater and greater faith.

Once you know what you want (Step I), and are practicing pretending you already have it (Step II), then the only thing left to do is:

Let it go and let it come to you.

This is the essence of Step III. Step III of The Formula is essentially all about *letting go and cultivating a consciousness of openness and receptivity*. There are two components to Step III: **technique** and **self-management**.

Technique addresses the technique of letting go and *self-management* addresses managing the human tendencies that hinder you in letting go. Learning techniques for letting go is relatively easy. But actually doing the techniques can be rather difficult because part of the human condition includes natural human tendencies, instincts and states of consciousness that grab our attention and serve to **distract** us from who we really are and what our souls really want. When we understand these "attraction distractions" and learn tools to prevent self-sabotage, we open our lives up to the infinite abundance of the Universe.

The Attraction Distractions

The Ego

In the discussion regarding being a multidimensional being, you were offered the perspective that there is a broader aspect of you, a broader aspect of your consciousness that operates in both your physical world *and* the realm of the absolute. The flip side of that addresses the part of you that perceives from a narrower physical perspective. That aspect of your consciousness is your ego. The ego is necessary for it allows you to perceive and foster the illusion that you are separate, an individuation of Source. The positive aspect of this is that, from this illusion of separation, you are able to experience time and space as we know it in this third-dimensional reality. It is this illusion that makes contrast and variety possible. And from this contrast, you are able to birth your desires, experiencing that which you want and that which you don't want. The challenge of the ego perspective is that, with this illusion of separation, you can also feel alone and separate from Source – *your* source of infinite well-being. It is this state of consciousness that requires self-management.

When you operate from your ego, you live from your five senses *only*. You react and respond to the conditions of your life from physical, emotional, mental and psychological perspectives. When you operate from the broader aspect of you, your ego actually works *with* your soul, which has access to the realm of the absolute. You use your five senses, yet you draw from your intuition as well. You react and respond to your world, but are able to observe your reactions. You not only access your physical, emotional and mental resources, but you also access spiritual and psychic resources. In other words you tap into higher guidance. You allow your actions and reactions to be guided from an inspired place, from a higher source of wisdom.

The *self-management opportunity* with the ego is to acknowledge that you are more than your ego. You are greater than the conditions of your life. You are not alone; you are a part of something bigger and grander. When you are feeling alone, afraid or overwhelmed by the third-dimensional world, the management opportunity is to remember that you have access to a power greater than your mind or body, greater than logic or luck. And if you can remember this, then you can access that greater power through the *techniques* of Step III, which we will be addressing a little later on.

Emotions

We all have emotional energy, and that emotional energy is here to serve us. But many of us have little idea how to use our emotional reactions in our favor. As a human tendency, our emotions become things that either control us or that we try to control. Many of us have no idea that emotions are the language of the soul. Many of us do not realize that, with the right context and understanding, our emotions can actually be the doorway to our higher guidance.

The *self-management opportunity* that lies in our human tendency to relate to our emotions from a context of control is to develop a relationship with our emotions that is based in honor, respect and wisdom. We will be delving into just exactly how to do that later in this chapter.

Limiting Belief Systems

We all have beliefs we have internalized as *truth,* but which are not truth. They are simply beliefs we've inherited or adopted. They form the boundaries and limitations to what we will allow ourselves to experience and have in our lives. These limiting belief systems must be identified and deconstructed so that a broader consciousness, based in truth, lets us allow more of the good that is our birthright into our experience. Some common limiting belief systems include: "I'm not good enough," "I'm damaged goods," "I'm imperfect," "I'm not loved," "I'm unlovable," "There is not enough (love, money, time …)," "I must earn it," "I don't deserve it," and, "I'm unworthy."

Did you notice that these limiting beliefs are declarative statements? Do they sound familiar? Like affirmations? Well, they *are* affirmations – *negative* affirmations. And when you have thoughts that you've been repeating to yourself for a long time, they become beliefs. They become all you know, so they feel like truth. But they are not truth.

The *self-management opportunity* with limiting beliefs is to recognize them for what they are. If you are thinking or feeling negatively about something to such a degree that you just can't shake it, it means you've internalized certain thoughts as truths. Once you realize that what you're focused on is not based in truth, you can begin to examine and ultimately dismantle your beliefs so they lose the power you've given them through repetition, through collecting evidence on behalf of the beliefs, and through the emotional energy you've poured into them.

Attachment

Attachment is the opposite of letting go. It is the feeling that has us hold on tightly to a person, situation or thing we feel we *must* have. It is a common reaction based on the idea, conscious or unconscious, that happiness and fulfillment come from things, people and conditions outside ourselves. When we are attached to something, we make that external thing our source, rather than turning within to our true Source. When we look outside ourselves for our fulfillment, we are in essence telling ourselves we are not whole, that our wholeness is outside ourselves and that we are separate from our wholeness. When we are attached to outside things, we are looking outside of ourselves to fill in the holes inside ourselves. Attachment comes from the internal drive to feel, remember and experience our wholeness. But it comes only from looking within to Divine Spirit to experience the wholeness that is already there.

The *self-management opportunity* that arises when you are feeling attached to something is to practice the art of letting go. At times, letting go can be incredibly difficult. Believe me, I understand! I am not speaking hypothetically when I remember feeling utterly hopeless over meeting Mr. Right and having a well-meaning friend cheerily advise me, "Let it go, and then he'll come to you." Or better yet, when I struggled with infertility for two years and cried month after month, and another well-meaning friend would tell me of couples who finally conceived when they "let it go." I wanted to punch her in the face. The thing about letting go is that you cannot let IT go unless you have something ELSE to take hold of when you do. That something else is Spirit. To effectively manage waves of attachment, you must practice what I call "replacement therapy." You replace the *thing* you *think* is your source with your *true* Source — over and over and over again.

Now Then ...

Before we move into the hows of managing our human tendencies, instincts and states of consciousness, let's first explore some basic techniques for letting go and being open and receptive. These techniques will deepen the understanding that will fuel your faith – the crux of Step III. As your faith is solidified in understanding, *Stepping Out of Your Own Way* to allow Infinite Intelligence to work its magic will become more integrated into your way of living.

Once you've got this foundation in place, then managing the human tendencies, instincts and states of consciousness (which will continue to show up as long as you're human) will become easier and easier. For example, your ego might come a-knockin' and you'll feel separate from the source of all supply. So you'll reach into your bag of tricks and manage your ego. Or your fear will show up and you'll think, "Oh, hello, fear, you again, huh?" And you'll pull a few tricks out of your hat to manage that. Or your limiting beliefs will have you believe that what you want is impossible, so you'll dismantle the beliefs and remember that *anything* is possible. Or your attachment will get the better of you and you'll pull out another set of tricks and find yourself breathing easier as you surrender and let go.

But, before I hand over the bag of tricks, let's learn more about letting go ...

12

Technique for Letting Go

"To truly find God, truth needs to be found independently from
the opinions of others. The truth has to be found in our hearts."
— *A.H. Almaas (1944 -)*
author, teacher, philosopher

Replacement Therapy

There is essentially one and only one technique for letting go,
and that is *replacement therapy*, which is to replace the thing you
think is your source (your dream, your desire, the thing you want)
with your *true Source*. Now, you may ask, "What exactly am I
letting go of?" Good question. When you *let go and let it come to
you*, you are letting go of all the things you cannot control. You
are letting go of how it comes to you and when it comes to you.
You are even letting go of the thing itself because when you manifest with The Mystic's Formula, you are choosing to fly instead
of walk toward your dream. And when you fly, you allow a force
greater than you to lift you up and carry you. That means you
don't need to know the details; Source handles that. And even
though you may *think* you know what you want, Source *really*
knows better than you what you want. Source will always give
you the *best possible version* of what you want if you allow it.
When you let go of the *thing* itself, you are allowing *it or something better* to come into your experience.

For replacement therapy to work well, you must identify for
yourself a concept, a construct, a notion, an idea, of a *thing* that

is *more* than you, or at least the mere mortal you, which you can turn to when you are letting go. This *thing* must make you *feel* good when you think of it. This *thing* is your *true source*. It must be unconditional. It must be all-good, all-loving, all-forgiving, all-knowing, all-powerful and eternal. Now, I can tell you that God is this. I can tell you that Source is this. I can tell you that Infinite Intelligence, Divine Spirit, Goddess is this. But until you discover how this could possibly be true for you, it won't matter what I tell you. You must have and cultivate a very personal relationship with Source, one based in *your* truth.

The tricky thing is, although surveys show that the great majority of people do believe in a higher power, our beliefs or lack thereof about this higher power may very well be based in things above and beyond *our own truths*. You may have already embarked on the journey of developing this very personal relationship I'm talking about. Or, you may not have done this work yet, in which case, your beliefs may be based in what you have been taught or adopted without further exploration. Your ideas, constructs and notions about God may *not* be based in *your* truth, but in *other people's truths*. And remember? We as people have those charming human tendencies, instincts and states of consciousness that limit our ability to experience freedom and fulfillment. As a result, the ideas you may have internalized about God *could be limited ideas*.

For example, ideas about God that are reflections of **ego issues** such as power and control *might* leave you feeling less than free in your relationship with God. Ideas about God that are reflections of **emotional issues** such as fear *might* leave you feeling afraid of God. Ideas about God that are reflections of **attachment issues** *might* make it difficult for you to *let go* and be *open and receptive* to new ideas about God (i.e., "My God is the right one and yours is not"). Ideas about God that are reflections of **limiting beliefs** *might* make it difficult for you to perceive God in any way other than what you know through your five senses or what you were taught.

If you do not have a notion of a higher power that is 100% safe to turn to, you will not be able to practice replacement therapy. Your source must be that safe haven you turn to when you let go – over and over and over again – of those things you desire most and the things you cannot control. If your ideas about God scare you, or make you feel bad, how do you expect to let go of the grip the conditions of your humanity have on you and turn your trust over to a conditional higher power?

Developing Your Very Personal Relationship with Source

> "Never lose a holy curiosity."
> — *Albert Einstein (1879-1955)*
> *physicist*

To cultivate a relationship with God means more than simply identifying **your truth** (i.e., your definition of God and your beliefs). As is the case with human relationships, in order to develop a truly satisfying relationship with God, you must be willing to give and receive. You must be willing to give of yourself through risking – risk revealing all of you to another (God) who you have yet to discover, risk trusting when you do not yet know if you can trust, risk loving when you fear you may be hurt or disappointed, risk asking when you do not know if your asking will be heard, and risk wanting when you fear your want may not be answered. And as you continue to bring yourself to the relationship as fully and openheartedly as you can, facing the unknown, you must also be willing to receive the other (God) into your heart, into your mind and into your life. This requires an openness, willingness, patience and receptivity you may have never before accessed. You must be willing to listen with more than your ears and your intellect. You must listen with your body and be willing to *feel* God. You must listen and receive with your intuition and *sense* God. You must be willing to receive by *experiencing* God, by acknowledging the ever-present blessings that touch your life in the infinite expressions that show up – a phone call, a hug, a smile, a tree, a breeze, a moment of silence, an inspiration or a wave of peace or understanding.

And as you develop this relationship, you will discover an intimate experience of communication with Source and you will learn that Divine Guidance speaks to you in a very personal way and in a way that feels very different than other voices that may influence your life, such as the voice of fear, the voice of your ego, the voice of your parents or the voice of societal expectations. The voice of Spirit is still, quiet, clear, simple, often quick (like a flash of knowing or inspiration) and non-argumentative. And the first step to beginning this communication is willingness. You need only decide that you want this relationship and simply declare it to yourself and the Universe. Set forth your intention and state your willingness to having the highest truth of **your** relationship with God reveal itself to you. The rest will follow.

Helpful Hints for Developing Your Relationship with Source

"I am satisfied that when the Almighty wants me to do or not do any particular thing, He finds a way of letting me know it."
— *Abraham Lincoln (1809-1865)*
16ᵗʰ President of the United States

There is no *right* way to relate to God, only **your** way. Your relationship with God is a personal, sacred and intimate experience. I have found there are some things that, no matter how hard you try, you just can't put them into words. And to even try somehow seems to minimize the experience, such as trying to tell someone what it feels like to have a child, to suffer the loss of a loved one, to be in "the zone" as you step up to bat or when you surrender your one voice to the harmonic ocean of a hundred others in choir. Developing your relationship with God is *your* journey. And although there are wonderful teachers and resources out there to help you on your way, only you can take this journey. No one can do it for you.

And so, what follows are a few guidelines to help you on your journey. The best advice I can give you is to trust more in how you *feel,* and less in what you *think.* This advice goes for your ever-unfolding experiences along the journey, as well as for any teacher, book or class you may experiment with along the way. Trust how you feel. Keep checking in with your gut.

Listen for that still small voice of divine guidance, and **your** unique relationship with God will reveal itself to you.

Contemplation

To contemplate means to think and feel, think and feel, think and feel ... Contemplation is one method of exploration that can open doors to the discovery of your relationship with God. In order to contemplate, you must have something to contemplate upon. Anything that will stimulate your thinking will do the trick: books, audio programs, television, movies, classes or conversations with others. When new ideas are presented to you, your thinking will be stimulated. Let yourself have the time and space to ponder these thoughts. Explore them fully. See if you agree, disagree or just don't know. But don't just stop at the level of cerebral analysis. As you think about these things, keep bringing your attention to your heart and your gut and ask yourself, "How do I feel about these thoughts and ideas? Do they feel good, comforting, soothing, true? Do they feel bad to me, disturbing, agitating, incorrect, wrong?"

When you're feeling how these thoughts feel, try suspending judgment. Try creating a space where you can simply *be* with everything you are contemplating. Try letting go of *knowing* whether something is right or wrong, true or incorrect. Simply *be* with it and listen for the still, small voice of divine guidance. It may speak to you during your contemplations, or at another time when you least expect it. Divine guidance often communicates to you when you're not trying, when you've let go. The more you can create mental spaces of being, the more you allow the voice of divine guidance to be heard. As you contemplate thoughts and ideas about God, thinking and feeling your way, you will discover an unfolding of what is true for you.

Stillness/Meditation

There are many teachers and resources available for those who would like to learn how to meditate. There are different styles of meditation and different experiences to be had with meditation. Personally, I've benefited greatly from the practice, but I can also tell you that finding a way to enjoy and feel comfortable with meditation did not come easily to me. I've discovered this is true for some. There are those who can read a book or take a class, and they take to meditation like a fish to water. Then there are others who struggle with it. Oftentimes those who struggle are so caught up with "doing it right" that they can't seem to get beyond judging their attempts as failure. Maybe they fell asleep, or couldn't sit still for more than five minutes, or their minds wouldn't stop running with to-do lists or worries, or they didn't experience Nirvana or some kind of epiphany the first time out.

There is no question that meditation can be your portal to connecting with the divine. And so it is highly worth trying as you journey forward in your exploration of your personal relationship with God. Try some books, classes or teachers. Try it on for size. And if your first attempts don't cut it, try some different books, classes or teachers. You don't have to pursue meditation to the point of perfection, but it behooves you to stay open to having the possibilities of meditation reveal themselves over time.

My first attempts at meditation were in my early 20s. As I mentioned, I was one of those who just couldn't do it. Although I'd try here and there over the years, I had come to the conclusion that closed-eye meditation must not be *my* way of connecting with God because I felt so darned uncomfortable and antsy every time I tried. One of my healers told me that walking and other activities can be like meditation for some people. When I heard that, I knew that was me. So, I decided that I was a *walking meditator*. During my walks, I would feel free and peaceful. I would receive flashes of inspiration. My racing mind would calm. And I would experience feelings of connection to something bigger and grander than me and my life. In my 30s, I continued to give sitting meditation a try here and there. I started studying various forms of energy healing that required meditation. I was the recipient of many energy healings as part of my education as well as part of my own transformation. I have no doubt that energy healings contributed to my ability to sit in mediation, and, if that speaks to you, energy work may be one of the resources you explore. Yet beyond that, it is in the most recent years that I have come to understand two simple yet powerful concepts about meditation that seem to make all the difference in my ability to do it, enjoy it and gain value from it.

"We are human beings not human thinkings."
— *Deepak Chopra (1946-)*
medical doctor and New Thought leader

The first concept came one day when I happened upon a television show called *Soul of Healing*, featuring Deepak Chopra. Among many other things, he was teaching about meditation and talked about the importance of it and how to do it, but when he said the words, "We are human beings not human thinkings," I GOT IT. For all the times I had been so caught up with the *technique of meditation*, trying to *do it right*, judging my experiences as *wrong*, I could never seem to give myself permission to have whatever experience I would have and simply *be*. These words gave me permission, so thereafter, when I'd try to meditate, my only intention was to simply *be* – exactly how I was, exactly where I was, regardless of technique, no matter what my mind did or didn't do, no matter what my experience with the meditation was. When I began to meditate in this way, I experienced a new level of communication and connection with Divine Spirit, and I discovered another simple, yet powerful concept about meditation that has also made all the difference.

You are simply creating a space. That's it. That's all meditation is. I found that the focus of meditation was *not* about how to breathe correctly, or how to sit correctly, or what I do or don't do with my thoughts. When I had taken meditation classes in the past, that always seemed to be the focus. So, I misunderstood those technicalities to be the keys to a powerful meditation experience. I thought, if I do this just right, I'll learn to enjoy meditation like so many others. I also misunderstood what it meant to meditate *on* something. I used to hear people say, "I'm going to meditate on this," or, "I meditated on that." I thought that to meditate on something meant to choose a topic and, while sitting in meditation, to focus intensely on it as if focusing on the topic would somehow reveal some eternal truth about the subject at hand, and boy, did that turn out to be a frustrating experience. However, as I maintained my intention to *simply be* when in meditation, I discovered that answers were coming to me! I didn't have to *do* anything right. I didn't have to *focus* on anything *enough*. All I did was *sit and be*. And insights came to me – sometimes in the meditation, sometimes later on. And what I sensed was that I was simply creating a space. It was as if in the letting go of everything, and coming into the moment to simply BE, I opened a door from my physical world to the world of Spirit. I understand now that this experience was the cumulative effect of many years of reading and listening to others talk, teach and share about meditation. But, boy, when I got this, it opened up a whole new reality.

Pretending You Already Have It

Another way you may want to explore your developing relationship with God is to implement some of the skills and understandings you may have already gleaned through The Mystic's Formula. Identify what you want in your relationship with God and pretend you already have it. As you go through your day, when you think of God, focus on what you want, not what you don't want. Focus on what you have, not the seeming lack. Find a role model or example of someone who has a relationship with God that you wish to emulate and *pretend* you embody those feelings and qualities a little every day. Or as you lie in bed at night, *pretend* you already have the relationship with God you dream of and *act as if* – maybe talk to God, pray, light a candle or create some ritual. Remember The Mystic's Formula. Start with what you know about manifesting and lean on that to bring forth your creative energy behind this intention.

Letting Go of Pictures

"For me, God is personal in the sense that He affects every individual differently. The rabbis of the Midrash said, 'God is like a mirror. The mirror never changes but everyone who looks at it sees a different face.'"

— *Harold Kushner*
prominent American rabbi, author

A picture is a mental image of how you think something is *supposed to be*. As with any goal or dream, developing your personal relationship with God can be inhibited by *pictures*. Pictures are like fears, beliefs and expectations in that they can limit your ability to stay open to other possibilities. You may have the idea that you must go to church to develop your relationship with God, or meditate, chant religiously or pray every night in order to have a relationship with God. However, you may not be fulfilling your self-imposed expectations, in which case you may be cutting yourself off from acknowledging how you already *do* connect with God. Remember your relationship with God is *your* relationship with God. It is unique, personal and sacred. So, as you open up to discovering the truth of this for yourself, it behooves you to suspend judgment and remain open and receptive to new possibilities. You may connect with God through enjoying nature, or boating, journaling or walking. Some people connect with a unique *feeling* when they are swimming, gardening or feeding ducks at a pond.

As you let go of pictures and cultivate an attitude of openness and receptivity, you'll want to pay attention, once again, to how you feel. Because the essence of Divine Spirit is love, freedom, peace, joy, harmony, ease, grace, knowing, truth, expansion, infinite power, etc., you'll know you are connecting with God when you feel more of these kinds of feelings. And so it follows that if you feel peaceful, joyful and harmonious when you are gardening, then this may be a wonderful venue for exploration in your relationship with God. If you feel free, expansive and joyful when you're sailing, maybe this would be a place to return to as you develop your relationship with Source. If you feel easy, powerful and love-filled amidst nature, then nature may be the place to return to as you explore the possibilities. These types of settings can play host to your personal *God Time*.

What Then?

So, let's say you've found your *God Time*. Then what? How do you take the relationship further? Well, first and foremost remember: *simply be and allow a space*. That's a great place to start. Then once you've set that intention you can:

- Contemplate – thinking and feeling upon a particular topic.
- Set forth the intention to receive guidance regarding a particular subject in your life. Then just be, let it go, listen and trust that the answer is there and you will receive it.
- Set forth the intention to feel God, know God, experience God, express God in the most fulfilling way possible. Then just be, let it go, and trust.
- Ask questions and allow the space for answers to come. Then just be, let it go, listen and trust that the answer is there and you will receive it.
- Call upon qualities you need at the time: strength, or peace or clarity, then just be (exactly where and how you are at that very moment), let it go and trust.

Have you noticed a theme? Pretty obvious …

Just be.
Let it go.
Listen.
Trust.

These instructions could be called practices or disciplines and they, along with some others, are invaluable in cultivating your own, very personal relationship with God. You'll notice that they can only be done in a state of *beingness*. When you're cultivating your relationship with God, your energy is much more directed to *being* versus *doing*. And, any doing that you do comes from the guidance and inspiration you receive when being. Further on, you'll notice that the practices you draw upon as you explore techniques for letting go will also be powerful as you explore *Techniques for Managing Your Human Tendencies, Instincts, and States of Consciousness*, which is discussed in depth in the next chapter.

13

Technique for Being
Open and Receptive

Ask and It Is Given

It's true! Ask and it IS given. But just because it is given doesn't mean you're in a place to *receive* it. You are asking and being given what you ask for all the time, because *like attracts like*, because you're a walking magnet. But, if you are not in a place to *receive*, your dreams could very well be lining up outside your door, waiting for the day you'll open the door so they can all come walking into your life.

About Receiving

When I say, "Let it go and let it come to you," I'm not talking about just sitting around waiting for your dream to come to you. I'm talking about cultivating a consciousness of openness and receptivity. It is this consciousness that allows divine guidance to inspire your actions and orchestrate the details that will bring your dream into your experience. Being open and receptive is about being in the right energetic vibration to allow your dream in, but it's more than that. When you are open and receptive, you are able to let your soul guide you every step of the way toward your dream, through gut feelings, intuitive nudges, "aha" moments, synchronicities, uncanny "coincidences" and "chance" meetings.

Follow Your Bliss

"Follow your bliss" is a term coined by Joseph Campbell, the American professor of mythology. It means, "Let those things that bring you joy lead you." When we allow ourselves to be lead by that which brings us joy, what we're doing is seeking out that which makes us feel good and bringing our attention to it, with mind and heart. When we do this, we naturally feel good, which means our vibration becomes higher. When our vibration becomes higher, we allow a greater degree of Source Energy to move through us. And the more Source Energy we allow to move through us, the more we become vibrationally aligned with our desires.

This may sound simplistic, but if you consciously evaluate what you **follow** with your conscious mind, you'll become aware of how much and how often you allow yourself to be lead by those things that do *not* bring you joy. **Wherever the mind goes, the heart will follow. And wherever your heart goes, so go your emotions and so follows your vibration.** When you follow your bliss, you are consciously choosing to look for things to focus on that make you happy. When you follow your problems, concerns, worries or fears, you are choosing (consciously or not) to focus on things that make you feel bad.

When you consciously choose to follow your bliss, you begin to act much like a satellite dish, scanning the airwaves for the *joy frequency*. In other words, you start looking for thoughts that feel good. Once you find an object of your joy, you *lock on* and *tune in* to its signal. This means you are focusing on that thing, thinking about it and beginning to *feel* about it. As you feel good, your vibration is on the rise. And once your vibration is high, you move into that state of openness and receptivity. Finding ways to feel good is one of the most powerful things you can do to cultivate a consciousness of openness and receptivity. And the amazing thing is, *it doesn't matter what you're feeling good about.* As long as you're feeling good about anything, you're keeping the door open for your dream to come to you.

Two Job Descriptions

Another way to cultivate a consciousness of openness and receptivity is to understand the difference between *your* job and *the Universe's* job. Very simply, your job is to identify *what* you want and to be a vibrational match for it so you can receive it into your life. The Universe's job is to handle all of the details – the *how* part of making it all happen. **One of the quickest ways to shut down the openness and receptivity portal is to start thinking that you are supposed to figure it all out, handle the details and make it happen.** As soon as you shift into this state of consciousness, you can be pretty sure you're now operating from a more limited *motivational* place rather than allowing the full breadth of power that comes from the *metaphysical* approach. In other words, you may find yourself relying more heavily on action and analysis. You may find your ego taking over where your emotional reactions to third-dimensional conditions, limiting belief systems and attachments can get the better of you. If however, you fulfill your job description (versus attempting to fulfill the Universe's job description), you put your attention and energy into knowing *what* you want, feeling good any way you can, and letting go, over and over again, so you can remain open and receptive to that which the Universe has already given.

When you are doing your job well, you are:
- **Trusting** that the Universe is handling the details.
- **Watching and listening** for inspiration and guidance regarding any actions you need to take to move toward what the Universe has lined up for you.
- **Taking action** – *inspired* action.
- **Managing** your human tendencies, instincts and limiting states of consciousness.

Tools to Help You Do Your Job Well

- **Remember God First.** Divine Spirit is the beginning and the end of All That Is. If you find yourself impressed with or engaged in the conditions of your life, remember that all of it is *secondary* to Source. No person, place or condition is your Source. God is. Your third-dimensional reality is simply the manifestation of thoughts and emotions that were offered in the past. Your point of power is NOW, for your NOW is creating your reality. And the best way to harness your thoughts and emotions in the most expansive way possible is to turn to God first. Remember God's true nature. Contemplate it. Feel it. Affirm that God is your Source – your only, your every, your all.

- **Turn the other cheek to conditions and circumstances that are contrary to your desire.** Remember the concept of *thumbing your nose at the third dimension?* Well, you just can't practice this skill enough. There will **always** be things happening in your world you don't want, don't agree with, and **worst of all that you deem as a sign your dream is not happening – which is simply not true.** The third dimension does what the third dimension does. It demonstrates the energy that has been put forth *previously*. Period. When, for example, yet another relationship has failed, it is **not a sign** that you are doomed never to have a successful relationship. It is just the third dimension manifesting for you the energy you put forth previously as thought and emotion. One of the quickest ways to constrict your state of openness and receptivity is to take something *bad* that has happened and attach to it the *erroneous meaning* that more of it is your destiny. When you do this, you have just limited what you will allow the Universe to give you by judging the circumstances as bad, AND you've set into motion the creation of more of what you do *not* want, by putting lots of limiting beliefs and negative emotion into the manifestation machine. When undesired things happen in your third dimensional world, the best thing to do is turn the other cheek and pull out your bag of tricks to start focusing on what you want, being in gratitude, and feeling good. This will keep you open and receptive.
- **Turn the other cheek to nay-sayers.** Nay-sayers are people who rain on your parade, burst your bubble, take the wind out of your sail, see the glass as half empty,

and/or are highly proficient at expressing the voices of fear, doubt and pessimism. There will always be nay-sayers. But you don't have to listen to them and you don't have to give them any power. If a nay-sayer offers you any dose of negativity, simply say in your mind, "Thanks for sharing," and turn toward someone who will support you on your journey.

- **Build your own personal cheerleading team.** Cultivating and turning to your own personal cheerleading team can help tremendously in doing your job well. To strengthen your ability to remain open and receptive, you'll want to seek out like-minded and like-hearted people for support, inspiration and understanding. These are the people to listen to and give your attention and energy. Listen only to your cheerleading team. If you allow nay-sayers to get under your skin, your vibration will drop and so will your level of openness and receptivity. If you allow only your cheerleaders under your skin (and into your heart), you'll keep that openness and receptivity channel tuned right in.

14

Self-Management

"Sometimes life's shadows are caused by our standing
in our own sunshine."

— *Ralph Waldo Emerson (1803-1882)*
American author, poet, philosopher

Of course, every chapter in this book is an important piece of
the whole. But this particular chapter has got to be the
most determining factor regarding the degree of success you will
experience as a conscious creator. The reason for this is that, up
until now, you could conceivably read along, thinking, "Yeah.
Uh-huh. I get it. No problem. That makes sense. Got it. Yep.
Easy. I can do that." However, the techniques in this chapter
include the tools you need to really *integrate* all this information into your daily life – to really make the leap from, "These
are interesting concepts," to, "I know how this stuff works and I
use it in my daily life," and, "I experience the positive results
every day."

There is no escaping it. We are human beings. And for human beings, our egos, our emotions, our attachments and our
limiting beliefs can be our greatest challenges. You may or may
not be ready or willing to take on the commitment necessary to
manage your natural human tendencies, instincts and states of
consciousness. And if you're not, that's okay. It's no small commitment. It can be challenging and requires mindfulness and
effort. But you should at least understand that it's not neces-

sarily any easier to live the life you lead *without* this commitment. Living life, feeling like a powerless victim of circumstance, is no easier or better than the alternative – really getting it about your power, owning it and developing your mastery of its use.

In his book, *SuperBeings,* John Randolph Price has a wonderful chapter that describes 12 progressive states of consciousness as we expand in our awareness of our creative power as individualized expressions of Infinite Intelligence. He describes how the journey of raising our awareness can evolve from a degree of *unconsciousness,* where we may feel "done to," or at the mercy of circumstances and fate, through different stages of awakening, where we begin to understand our true nature, and how to manifest our power in our experience. In the earlier stages of consciousness, you may understand the basic concepts, but they remain conceptual or intellectual. So, you may not necessarily feel a sense of urgency about managing your human tendencies. However, as your consciousness expands, you begin to experience, in more and more pronounced ways, the consequences of choosing, or not, to harness your power. Consequently, you begin to awaken to the notion that you simply do *not* have the luxury to live life *hanging out* in your ego consciousness without taking responsibility for what you're creating in your life. Living from an ego consciousness lends itself to:

- Operating from a place of reactivity to your third-dimensional reality.
- Wallowing in fear, anger, resentment, blame or victimhood.
- Resting in your limiting belief systems without challenging them.
- Allowing yourself to suffer in the prison of attachment without at least trying to find ways to let go.

Meeting Your Witness

God may have given you human attributes that can feel tremendously challenging at times, but God also gave you a superhuman instrument with which to manage those limiting human tendencies, instincts and states of consciousness. That instrument is *your witness*, and it is the part of you that can *observe* yourself. Spiritual teacher and author, Eckhart Tolle, teaches that for each of us, there is an *I* and a *Me*. *Me* lives my life, reacting and responding to my environment. *I* watches *Me* living my life. *I* is able to *notice* – notice what *Me* is doing, feeling and thinking, and notice what my motivation is and what I'm trying to accomplish. That part of you that notices, the *I*, is your witness – the *I Witness* to all the choices you make, conscious and unconscious. The key to using your witness in a helpful and powerful way is to suspend judgment of anything in particular. *You simply notice.*

For example:

- You're paying your bills and once again, it doesn't feel like there's enough money. Your stomach gets tied up in a knot, you feel your jaw clench, your breathing becomes shallow, or maybe you just avoid the whole thing, go watch TV, leave the house, or rack up some more debt on your credit cards. When you call upon your witness, you no longer simply react to your debt. You also notice your reactions. You think or say to yourself, "Hmm, isn't that interesting. I'm paying my bills and I *feel* anxious. I *think* there's not enough. I *react* to my conditions, rather than *act* from wisdom."

- You're having another horrible day at work. You're hating your job and are thinking about finding another job, or better yet, starting that mechanic business you've always dreamed of. You get depressed because that kind of change feels impossible. You continue your job as your ulcer gets more painful and you pop another four Ibuprofen because your neck and shoulders are killing you. When you call upon your witness, you pull yourself out of your stress and mindfully observe your thoughts, "Hmm, isn't that interesting. There seems to be a pattern. I hate my job. It makes me physically sick, but every time I start to even think about finding a solution to change this situation, I quit before I even start. I *feel* and *act* like a total victim. I *feel* guilty when I think about trying to do something that makes me happy when I still need to provide for my family. I *think* I don't know how or where to begin. Hmm, isn't that interesting?"

- You've got yet another first date and you're already planning the wedding in your head. You're a nervous wreck, trying to anticipate what he'll think of you, what to say, what he'll say. You don't even know the guy, yet you're living in some completely fabricated future. You go on the date and feel awkward, weird and like a loser. He takes you home and you think, "What just happened?" When you call upon your witness, you put away the 2x4 you were beating yourself with and notice, "Hmm, isn't it interesting how I can't seem to just *be*. All this trying to control things and predict the future prevents me from being fully present. I *feel* nervous and scared. I don't even know what I'm scared of. I can't even get to know if I like the guy, cuz I'm too worried about if he likes me. And then another date goes by and I walk away *feeling* insecure, *acting* as someone other than who I really am, and *feeling* powerless to have a successful relationship."

Your witness never judges you, no matter how much your ego may want to. Your witness' power mantra is, "Isn't that interesting." And your witness' power skill is notice, notice, notice. **Once you are able to stand back and notice your natural human tendencies, instincts and states of consciousness when they are happening, THEN you use the following tools to manage your ego, emotions, limiting beliefs and attachments.** So, then … let's get a-managing!

15

Integrating Your Ego

"The facade is the ego. It is motivated by our seeking love. The only reward is frustration, as it is only by loving that one finds love."

— *Lester Levinson*
developer of The Sedona Method

In order to manage the challenges that can arise from your ego, you must first know what your ego looks and sounds like. You must also understand that managing your ego is not about making it *go away*. Unless you're one of the few who will evolve to the status of Ascended Being during this lifetime, you'll have your ego for the duration of your life. Remember, this section is about *managing* not *getting rid of* your ego needs.

When Your Ego Serves You

Your ego can be a really fun part of who you are. It's the part of you that sets you apart from others. The part of you that wants to be unique, separate, original and in charge. That wants to shine, be right, get credit and be acknowledged. It gets you moving, motivates you into action and helps launch your desires. When these qualities are in service to your soul's higher guidance, your ego serves you. Essentially, your ego is working in partnership with your soul. However, if your ego is flying solo and has taken charge of your life, these same attributes can cause you longing, suffering and the general malaise of *not enough-*

ness. In order to manage your ego when it's taking over, and things are not feeling or going so well, you must: a) recognize your ego when it's showing up (this is the job of your witness), b) accept it, and c) encourage your ego to step aside and allow your soul to take over the reigns of your life – at least for a while.

How to Recognize Your Ego

Recognizing your ego is a journey of expanding your awareness. I recall understanding the *idea* that I had an ego years before I actually *recognized* my ego. I remember, oh so well, that "aha" moment when I thought to myself, "Ooooooh, so THAT's what my ego looks like – ugh." Recognizing your ego can be quite tricky, for it doesn't always show up in the most obvious of ways. And although there are signs and expressions of ego that show up in behaviors, it takes more than that to become an effective ego-spotter.

When Your Ego Does Not Serve You

Your ego is that part of you that maintains the illusion that you are separate from Source. When you feel separate from Source, you feel alone. You disconnect from your source of love, safety and supply. So, your perspective moves into an illusory world of limitation – a world where supply of all things is finite, a world where love and support are conditional, a world where your self-perception is dictated by comparison to others and is based in a perception of limitation.

When you are caught in the illusion of ego, you will think you *are* your ego. Your ego will protect and defend you in your illusion of separateness. This means that when your ego is governing your consciousness and perception, you'll find yourself driven to be right or make your point at the expense of harmony in relationships. You'll find yourself driven to win at the expense of someone having to lose. You'll feel better about yourself when you think you are better than others. You'll crave external credit or acknowledgment at the cost of a deeper inner experience of fulfillment. You might find yourself feeling possessive or territorial, either because you believe there's not enough to go around, or because you need external things, which you attach to yourself to validate your worth. And in general, there will be a part of you that is insatiable, needing or wanting more, more, more because you feel there's never enough.

What It Looks Like When You Are Integrating Your Ego

When, however, you are integrating your ego, you're allowing yourself to remember your true nature by allowing your soul to govern your consciousness in partnership with your ego. When you let your soul into the picture, then you're connecting to Source. You are acknowledging that you're a part of a unifying ocean of energy that is infinite in love, safety and supply. You are willing to remember and call upon the truth that all is truly well and there really is enough – always. When you're living your life from this place, harmony becomes more important than being right. The internal fulfillment that comes from genuine self-expression is infinitely more satisfying than any award or pat on the back could be. You discover that the satisfaction of getting can't even compare to the rewards of giving. It becomes easy to be in gratitude because you're able to acknowledge that at all times there is more than enough. And you never feel alone because you know you never are. When this partnership is working well, it means you're integrating your ego into a broader definition of who you are and how you operate in the world.

Exercise

This analysis of ego is all well and good, but the tricky part is noticing and catching your ego in the act, so you can intervene and manage it when it is not serving you.

The following exercises provide effective ways to begin discovering what your ego looks, sounds and feels like. Allow yourself some time to really give yourself to the discovery process available through these exercises. There are three sections, which will allow you opportunities for exploration. You may want to spread the different sections out over days, weeks or longer, giving yourself time to digest, explore, feel and integrate.

Part I – Reflecting and Writing

In this exercise, you will consciously give voice to your ego. In order to recognize and manage your ego, you must accept it. So, as you proceed, give yourself the gift of suspending any and all judgment. Remember, we all have egos. And if we don't befriend our egos, they are destined to become our enemies.

Below are two fill-in-the-blank exercises. Complete the first one before you move on to the second one. To fill in the blank, allow yourself time for simply *being* with the statement. Allow yourself "stream of consciousness" writing. And when you hit silences, be in the silence. Let the information keep coming. It may not be a fast process, but the information will flow. Refrain from judging your answers. Just create a space for your truth to be revealed, just be, and let it flow. When you can't write anymore, move on to the second statement.

First statement:

> **I want people to think I am** _____. *(fill in the blank)*

Below are examples of responses to this exercise. Your list may not be this long. These are just ideas to help stimulate the discovery of your own truth.

I WANT people to think I am ...
- smart enough
- dependable
- responsible
- perfect
- competent
- a good friend
- a good listener
- capable
- of integrity
- successful
- intelligent
- powerful
- worthy of respect

- worthy of recognition
- worthy of love
- a good leader
- a force to be reckoned with
- deserving of nice things
- competent
- generous
- loving
- thoughtful
- normal
- cool
- funny

Remember to wait until you feel complete with this first statement before moving on to the second statement.

Second statement:

I DON'T WANT people to think I am _____.
(fill in the blank)

Below are more examples to help you discover your own answers.

I DON'T WANT people to think I am ...
- a spiritual, cosmic flake
- a wimp
- anal-retentive
- controlling
- a bitch
- too serious, significant and intense
- overwhelming to others
- irrational
- Pollyanna
- a jerk
- impatient
- intolerant
- irresponsible
- damaged goods

- a loser
- lonely
- hurt
- socially awkward
- a failure
- isolated
- depressed
- pathetic
- a drama queen
- negative
- stupid
- incompetent
- like all the others

Allow yourself to feel complete before moving on to Part 2.

Part 2 – Contemplation

Once you have completed Part 1, allow yourself some time and space to contemplate your responses. Remember, to contemplate means to think and feel, and think and feel, and think and feel. You may want to refer to the questions below to give you some more fuel for contemplation. Journaling your thoughts and feelings is another great way to explore and discover your truth.

- What am I trying to prove?
- Who am I trying to prove these things to?
- What if I am *not* the very things I want people to think I am?
- What would that mean?
- What would that say about me?
- What if I *am* the very things I want people to think I'm not?
- What would that mean?
- What would that say about me?
- Are any of these statements true about me or are they limiting beliefs? Are they judgments? Who is judging me?

Part 3 – An Exercise in Acceptance

The following section is an exercise in acceptance. When you accept something you have been resisting, it loses power over you. If you've been trying to prove you are or are not something, it means you have been maintaining a vibration that who you are, exactly as you are, is not enough. In other words, you have been in resistance. And you may recall that what you resist persists. As long as you're resisting any part of you, imagined or real, you are limiting your connection to Source, because you *are* Source! Remember? There is only One! So, as you accept all of you, you accept and allow more Source energy to move in, as, and through you. And the more room Source takes up inside you, the less room ego has.

After having contemplated who you want people to think you are and are not, you will be *reversing* each statement and *owning it* by turning it into a declaration. This will allow you to practice letting go of resistance and embracing the very things you've been resisting – even if only for a moment. Try it on for size. I promise, this has the potential to be quite liberating!

A. For each "I WANT people to think" statement – REVERSE IT and write the following:

I am NOT _____. *(fill in the blank)*

The following are examples of reversed statements made into declarations:
- I am NOT smart enough
- I am NOT dependable
- I am NOT responsible
- I am NOT error-free (i.e. I am NOT perfect)
- I am NOT competent
- I am NOT a good friend
- I am NOT a good listener
- I am NOT successful
- I am NOT capable
- Etc...

B. And, for each "I DON'T WANT people to think I am" statement - REVERSE IT and write the following:

I AM _____. *(fill in the blank)*

The following are examples of reversed statements made into declarations:
- I AM a spiritual, cosmic flake
- I AM a jerk
- I AM anal-retentive
- I AM a loser
- I AM a failure
- I AM controlling
- I AM a bitch
- I AM too serious, significant and intense
- I AM a wimp
- I AM overwhelming to others
- I AM irrational
- I AM Pollyanna
- Etc...

C. Time to Explore

Once you have your declarations, you have the opportunity to explore your ego further.

Your task is to read through each of your declarative statements from lists A&B above, four times out loud. After each statement, apply one of the four exploratory tools below.

As you do this, see how it feels. You may notice yourself releasing some resistance. You may feel an unusual, yet welcoming, feeling of acceptance washing over you. And you may discover altogether new questions about you and your life that give rise to new levels of self-discovery.

This section alone can be as in-depth as you want it to be. Some people may be inclined to follow this exercise to the letter, using each of the four exploratory tools. Others may find that just a few of the four tools are enough to shed profound light on their awareness of their ego and how it does and does not serve them in their lives. Trust yourself in this process and use the exercise in whatever way feels best to you.

Exploratory Tools

1. Could that statement be true? If so, could I consider accepting that about myself? If not, could I let go of the need to prove or disprove it?
2. Try turning the statements into questions (i.e., "What if I AM controlling? What would that mean? What would that say about me? Is that true or a belief?")
3. What happens when you follow the statement with "sometimes"? (i.e., "What if I'm not a good friend sometimes?")
4. What happens when you follow any given statement with "yet"? (i.e., "I'm not successful ... yet. I am not capable ... yet.")

What All of This Means

What often happens with this exercise is that you'll discover there is at least some truth, if not a lot of truth, to your declarative statements. When you can begin accepting the truth of who you are, in all of your glorious, imperfect humanity, then you've begun to **love** yourself. And when you love and accept yourself, then transformation can happen. Transformation and healing are not possible in an environment of resistance. This is because the very thing you wish were different will gain strength as you give it your negative attention through resistance.

These exercises give you an opportunity to come face to face with your ego, and become more conscious to an aspect of you that may unconsciously be more in control of your life than you realize. The more conscious you are of your ego-driven tendencies, the more power you have to take charge when your ego is not serving you. The more unconscious you remain, the more you may suffer at the mercy of your ego. By exploring the possibility of owning and releasing notions about who you think you are and are not, you begin to take back some of the power your ego may have in your life. You begin taking the charge off of these issues. You move further into self-acceptance, which has the capacity to fuel transformation.

Integrating your ego means noticing it, accepting it and knowing when it serves you and when it does not. When your ego serves you, enjoy it. Have fun with it. Allow it to be in service to your soul's guidance. When it doesn't serve you, then it's time to manage it. You manage it through self-talk. When it shows up and is not serving you, you'll know because you'll feel bad in one way or another. You may find yourself in scarcity thinking. You may feel possessive or territorial. Or craving credit or acknowledgment. Or driven to prove something or make a point. You may catch yourself putting all the attention on yourself, not listening to others, building a case, needing to be right. If any of these things are going on and you're feeling stressed, not enough, not appreciated, alone, judgmental, etc., then there's a good chance your ego has gotten the better of you and it's time to manage it.

Back to Replacement Therapy

So how exactly do you manage your ego when you have recognized it and it's not serving you? Well, this is when you go back to your replacement therapy. This is when you turn to Spirit and start talking and listening. Whatever it takes for you to connect with the broader perspective of you is what it takes to manage your ego. When your ego is in charge, you'll find you're probably holding on to something pretty tightly. This is the time to turn to God, so you *can* let go of the attachment, see things more clearly, and take direction from your soul. You'll know you're managing your ego well when:

- You're breathing more easily.
- You feel as if you've let go of the thing you were holding onto so tightly.
- You feel yourself remembering you're not alone, that God loves you and that if you allow it, you'll be guided to your greatest good.
- You find yourself more able to be in and enjoy the present moment, rather than having your body in one place and your mind in another.

You'll know you are managing *any and all* of your human tendencies, instincts and states of consciousness well, when you feel these ways. You might call this: "being in the God zone." When you're in the God zone, your soul has taken back the reigns of your life – taken back the reigns from your ego, from your attachment, from your emotions and from your limiting beliefs.

Short-Term vs. Long-Term Ego Management

This ongoing technique of noticing your ego when it shows up, assessing whether or not it is serving you, and practicing replacement therapy is a short-term solution to the problems your ego can present. It works, yet it requires constant mindfulness. There is a longer-term approach that can make the management of your ego much easier, and that approach is the pursuit and expression of your higher purpose in life.

Your soul came here to do something. Your soul, that broader, grander aspect of you, vibrates at a unique and original frequency. It has its own signature, which, like a fingerprint, only you have. To know your purpose is to know what your soul came here to do. Your soul has a unique calling, a passion, a need to express itself fully. And only you can offer what your soul has to offer. This drive for self-expression is expansive. The word *expand* is defined as: "to increase in extent, size, scope, or volume." Hence, when you are living from purpose, you are experiencing and expressing energies that go *beyond* you. You give. You offer. You express. You serve. You contribute. In other words, one way or another, you are reaching *others*. And because this all originates within the soul, and the soul is the conduit to the Universe and its natural essence of love, when you are living from higher purpose, the effect on others will always be positive.

When you know your purpose and have found satisfying ways to express it, you have walked through a door that is now forever open to you. Your consciousness has now expanded to accommodate a new way of living. And although your consciousness can always remember how to live life from ego, it now has an alternative perspective that is oh-so-much-more satisfying. The reason that living your life from purpose makes the management of your ego so much easier is that purpose is so much more powerful than ego. The expansive energies of higher purpose include energies like love, joy, creativity and gratitude. On the other hand, ego is aligned with energies like fear, separation, limitation and scarcity. It is an energy that contracts. Remember, ego is that part of your consciousness that maintains the illusion of separation from Source. Therefore, as opposed to serving *others,* ego is all about serving the *self* in maintaining and protecting the illusion of separation, aloneness and not-enoughness.

When your sense of self is rooted primarily in the ego, that is all you have to work with. So, if you want to manifest soulfully, you have to manage your ego on an ongoing basis. However, when your sense of self is rooted in higher purpose, suddenly a very expansive energy has taken over your persona. In essence, your higher purpose overpowers your ego. Your ego simply does not have the room, the time or the space to get the better of you, because your purpose is taking up most of your consciousness. When your purpose is alive and well, expressing in your life, managing your ego is infinitely easier.

Ego vs. Purpose

In an effort to shed more light on what it feels like to live from ego verses purpose, opposite are two lists that compare the consciousness of each. As you peruse these lists, make note of the phrases that ring true for you. This may help you see where in your life you live from ego and where you live from higher purpose.

A Few Examples

Below are a few examples that illustrate how ego and higher purpose can express in everyday lives.

The Higher Purpose Wife and Mother

Let's say you're a wife and mother who expresses your higher purpose through the love and care you give your family. When you are living your life from purpose, you are fulfilled. Oh sure, you may be running around, always busy, not getting much sleep, but generally your heart is overflowing. Your ego may show up

Ego	Purpose
Your ego is insatiable. It always needs more, more, more – more stuff, more attention, more money, more credit.	Your purpose overflows your heart with fulfillment, awe, gratitude and humility. Sometimes you feel like your heart can't hold it all.
Your ego wants to get or take.	Your higher purpose wants to give, share or offer.
Your ego's needs can leave you feeling tired, stressed, unsatisfied and afraid.	Your purpose energizes you, even if you're doing more and sleeping less.
Your ego wants you to accumulate personal achievements, and to get credit or acknowledgment for it.	Your purpose wants you to connect with others and to see results that benefit others.
Your ego is selective about what tasks it will and will not do.	Your purpose doesn't care what task you do. It simply wants to be of service.
Your ego makes *you* **want** even if you don't need.	Your purpose **wants you**. You feel a need to heed its call.
You can often feel your ego in your head.	You can often feel your higher purpose in your heart.
Your ego fuels your insecurities.	Your higher purpose heals your insecurities.

as resentments that you don't have time for yourself, that you feel invisible and that you're not getting credit for all you do. You may find yourself keeping score of what you do in comparison to your husband. However, when you are living from purpose, you are fully aware that the health and well-being of your family must guide you in all of your decisions and actions. So, rather than wallowing in the ego consciousness of needing to be right, withholding love, feeling sorry for yourself because no one appreciates you, you practice replacement therapy. You exercise your ways of connecting with Source, so that you may be guided in how to best honor your feelings, and be inspired to find solutions to the problems that feed your resentments. If, in contrast, you were a wife and mother living more from your ego, your personal needs would take precedence over the needs of your family, which could cost your family its health and well-being. A higher purpose mom nurtures her needs in ways that serve her family. A mom living from ego nurtures her needs at the expense of her family's needs.

The Higher Purpose Businessman

The higher purpose businessman will likely have many common interests and passions with the ego-driven businessman. He may be highly enthusiastic at the idea of creating a product that reaches a large audience, enjoy recognition in the form of acknowledgment and positive reviews, he likes making money and lots of it, loving the feeling of freedom, power and abundance. He enjoys feeling powerful in his world and with others. However, the higher purpose businessman differs from the ego-driven business man in that these experiences and conditions are only the beginning of something larger for him. All of these forms of self-expression and power are actually a means to a greater end. The power, the creativity, the abundance that he generates as an entrepreneur allow him to be and give more to others. It might come in the form of generous philanthropy, or he may create and manage his business as an expression and example of higher values that he would like to share with others – values such as generosity, trust, relationship and community. He takes on challenges that may arise in the course of doing business as an opportunity to discover or practice a higher principle aligned with his soul's truth. In contrast, the motivation of the ego-driven businessman begins and ends with the self. He defines himself by demonstrations of power, freedom, success, abundance and acknowledgment. He sees the successful conditions and events of his business as opportunities to *prove* something about who he is. As opposed to being sensitive to the longer-term and farther-reaching impact his actions and his business can have on others, he is focused primarily on how all things business-related affect the business itself and consequently him.

The Higher Purpose Artist

The higher purpose artist, like the higher purpose businessman, views her work as a venue for authentic self-expression and reaching others. She is called to create, to express, to communicate and to stimulate. She feels she really has no choice in how she spends her waking hours. Her soul tells her, "You must do your art." A life without art feels meaningless. For all higher purpose people, expressing their purpose gives their life meaning. In contrast, for the ego-driven artist, although these higher callings may indeed be a part of what moves the artist to do her work, the ego can become a point of conflict. The needs of the ego might drown out or distort the purity of the soul's communication through art. Ego gratification such as validation or financial compensation may overpower the initial call to create and express. And the issue of having to prove something can infect the creative process, leaving the artist disconnected and unfulfilled, or even wounded in her ability to produce artwork that touches others the way her soul desires.

The Higher Purpose Friend

The higher purpose friend considers the needs of her relationship in balance with her own needs. When challenges arise in the friendship such as hurt feelings, misunderstandings or disagreements, the higher purpose friend considers the long-term health of her friendship. She asks herself, "What does our relationship need?" as opposed to "What do I need?" The ego-driven friend may feel she needs her friend to call first, or she needs attention or an apology. She may be too consumed with her own perspective to stand outside herself to consider what may be going on for her friend. Her own needs blind her to the needs of her friendship, which could ultimately cost her the friendship. In contrast, the higher purpose friend, although she honors her own feelings, is able to risk trusting again when she's been hurt, is able to put aside her pride to call first, and is able to remember that her friend might be going through her own challenges, which cause her to be less emotionally available to her. The ego-driven friend attempts to get her needs met by *getting or taking* from the friendship, whereas the higher purpose friend seeks to give to her friendship, trusting that her needs can be met as a result of nurturing the relationship.

If I Don't Know What My Higher Purpose Is

> "Where your talents and the needs of the world cross,
> there lies your vocation.
> — *Aristotle (384 - 322 BCE)*
> *ancient Greek philosopher*

If you're thinking, "This long-term approach to managing your ego sounds just grand, but I don't know what my higher purpose is," fret not. Everyone has a higher purpose inside them, just waiting to be let out. There are lots of resources out there to discover your purpose – great books, classes and teachers. Ever heard the saying, "When the student is ready, the teacher appears"? Well, if you're ready, that's all it takes to set you on your path of discovery. All you need is the desire or the *wanting* to know, and the rest will follow, which brings us back to Step I of The Mystic's Formula, *Identify What You Want.*

If you want to know your purpose, first you must *let* yourself want it. Then, sink your teeth fully into Step I. You'll recall that there are numerous tools that are helpful in identifying what you want – *Noticing the Dissonance, The Detective Method, The Brainstorming Method, The Collage Method* and *The Vision Workshop.* And, although all of these techniques are helpful in different ways, **if you want to get really specific, if you want to be able to stand tall and declare your purpose in one clean, short sentence, then skip ahead to the *Vision Workshop* technique and fast-forward to the *Why* portion of the process. If you give yourself fully to that process, you'll come away knowing your purpose, no question about it.**

I Know My Purpose, But Don't Know How to Express It

It is not uncommon to know your purpose, but to avoid it, or to be lost as to how to take the necessary action to express it. This happens for many reasons. Sometimes fear gets the better of us. You may know your soul's calling, but are afraid to fail at something you care so much about. "What if I try this and can't do it? What will become of me, then? There's nothing else that I care about this much." And then there's always the fear of success. Many times we think, "If I succeed at this, then I'll have to do it all the time. I'll never get to rest, be lazy or focus on myself again."

Sometimes our fear looks like being overwhelmed. We think that because we know our life's purpose, we have to take it on all at once. We think we have to quit our jobs, or do our higher purpose full-time, or leap from obscurity to doing the talk-show circuit … something like that. When you find yourself paralyzed by all-or-nothing thinking, the first thing to remember is that *anything is better than nothing.* Let me make one thing perfectly clear: **You do not have to give up your current life to express your higher purpose.** And, one of the best mantras I've ever heard for those that struggle with overwhelm in *any* area of their lives comes from Mike Dooley, author of *Infinite Possibilities.* He teaches us to …

Do what you can.

This elegantly simple mantra is worth its weight in diamonds. If you practice no other affirmation but *Do what you can,* your life will transform. If you know your purpose, that which gives your life meaning, you're ahead of most people. However, there are many who know what gives their life meaning, but have never taken the next step, which is to actively engage in expressing it. An unfilled higher purpose is just that – *unfulfilling,* not to mention virtually useless in the longer-term management of your ego. As a matter of fact, your ego might be one of the culprits keeping your higher purpose safely hidden from all those who could benefit. But just because you know your higher purpose does not mean you have to express it full time, or make money at it, or quit your job, or do anything drastic.

For example, you may discover that your higher purpose is to "Be an example of a woman who fully embraces life," and your life may feel as full as it can be with a husband, children and work. In *doing what you can,* you may change nothing about your life but your attitude. In embracing that your purpose involves fully embracing life, you may have come to realize where and how you have *not* been fully embracing life. You may suddenly notice that you live in the future quite a lot, planning, and running to-do lists in your head. You may realize that because of this, you are rarely fully present in anything you do. Maybe with your kids, you spend too much time thinking about the laundry that isn't getting done or the report you need to finish for work. And then when you are at work, you spend a lot of time feeling guilty for not having enjoyed hanging out with your kids when you had the time. As you *do what you can* to express your higher purpose of being an example of a woman who fully embraces life, you commit to yourself that you will live *fully in the present moment!* When you're with your kids and husband, you fully give yourself the permission to simply BE with them. When you are at work, you give yourself fully to your work. You never have regrets or fear that precious time is slipping away, because you know you're living in the *now* as much as possible and you know that *now* is where life happens. Your work hours remain the same. You've taken on not a single volunteer hour. You have not sacrificed nor gained any pay, but something transformational has happened. By *doing what you can,* your children, your husband and your work colleagues are being blessed every day by your higher purpose.

Or your higher purpose may be to "Engage in the process of locating and expressing your fullest potential as a human being," and when you let yourself want what you want, you know that the lifelong fantasy of creating a national nonprofit youth empowerment center for inner-city boys is really your soul's full potential agitating your fear-based ego. You have a family to provide for. Bills to pay. Wouldn't know where to start. What do you do with this higher purpose? You *do what you can!* You first let yourself want what you want. Then you dare to share your dream with your wife, explaining that you don't know how this could ever happen, but you've got this dream. Then you research non-profits on the internet. Then you learn about a class on forming non-profits. Then you sign up for the class, etc., etc., etc.

One inspired action at a time, *you are expressing your higher purpose!* You do what you can. **You are successful in expressing your higher purpose, not when you've completed anything, but when every day, in some small way, the larger part of you, your soul, is doing something, *anything,* aligned with its calling.** The truth is, when you're living your higher purpose, you're never done. It's a state of being, a path you put yourself on. And as such, your ego gets pushed aside more and more because your ego cannot coexist with your higher purpose. Your higher purpose is always asking, "What more can I give, learn, express, offer?" Your ego is always asking, "What about me?" These two energies are mutually exclusive because when you're feeling the expansion of giving, the energy of taking hurts (figuratively and literally). The more you experience the fulfillment of purpose, the less you'll be seduced by the illusion of ego.

Staying Out of Your Own Way

In order to successfully practice Step III of the Mystic's Formula, you must practice ego-management. Whether you take on a short-term or long-term approach, mindfulness and awareness are vital. With willingness and practice, this discipline will become easier and more natural. Over time, you'll become adept at recognizing when your ego has taken control of your mindset. You'll remember that your ego has you believing in an illusion: that you are alone, that you are not enough, that you must fend for yourself and that you are separate from Source. By consistently practicing replacement therapy, your soul will guide you back to truth. You'll remember that you are loved, that your nature is well-being and abundance, and that you are one with Source.

16

Harnessing the Power
of Your Emotions

"By letting all emotions have their natural release, the 'bad' ones
are transformed to 'good' ones, and, in Buddhist terms, we are
then liberated from suffering."

— *Candace Pert, Ph.D.*
author, Molecules of Emotions:
The Science Behind Mind-Body Medicine

Through my travels, I have come to the conclusion that many,
many people have a relationship with their emotions that
is at best stilted or unconscious. This is a big problem because:
a) emotions are an unbelievable force in the creation of your
dream life, and b) if you are living out this life as a mere mortal,
with all the human trappings (as most of us are), life is an emotional prospect. There is no getting around it. And yet most of
us have a relationship with our emotions that is based on control. Either we are trying to control our emotions, or they are
controlling us. Or we are trying to stay in control by avoiding
them, suppressing them, distracting ourselves, or running away
from them. But to honor our emotions and to have the slightest
sense of what purpose they serve in our lives, not to mention
harnessing their power ... well, that is just not a commonplace
awareness.

This chapter is dedicated to debunking the myths and cor-
recting misinterpretations and misunderstandings regarding the

role and power of our emotions in our lives and as conscious creators. Although there are many tools you can study, experiment with and implement as you create the life of your dreams, I have discovered that the foundation of it ALL lies in having a healthy and productive relationship with your emotions. If you don't have that, you aren't going to get very far. It is the degree to which you can personally harness the power of your emotions that determines your level of mastery as a powerful manifestor in your own life.

Why is this? Because life in general, and the pursuit of your dreams, specifically, is an emotional proposition. Do these sentiments sound familiar?

- I was paralyzed by fear.
- I'm so nervous I want to puke.
- Why do I procrastinate about something so important to me?
- I really want to be rich, but I feel guilty.
- I can't understand why I keep sabotaging myself?
- She is drowning in grief.
- His rage consumed him.

All of these statements reflect how our emotions can be our greatest obstacles if we don't know how to harness their power. When you have a healthy relationship with your emotions, these potential blocks can become your greatest catalysts for success.

The Myth

Yes, we are indeed spiritual beings having a human experience. But I have noticed there is a common notion in the world of metaphysical study that has people feeling as if they are expected to skip the "human" part on the way to expressing their infinite spiritual nature as co-creators with Source. Whether the metaphysical teachings do not effectively address this issue or the teachings are being misinterpreted, the end result is that people become afraid of their emotions.

Here is what commonly happens: As we begin to awaken to our power as co-creators with Spirit, we learn that we create with our thoughts and emotions. And so when we inevitably have the human experience of thoughts and emotions that are contrary to what we wish to create, we try to *control* ourselves into thinking and feeling *correctly*. This makes people crazy! And it is actually counterproductive.

Let's face it, as spiritual beings having a human experience, our buttons get pushed. We react to life. Emotions, like your thoughts, are like electrical activity. They are energy. They exist. If you harness their energy, they will work for you. If you don't harness the energy, you can get hurt. Consider these human experiences:

- The lonely man from a broken home wants a loving wife and family.
- The single mother who can barely make ends meet dares to pursue a life of prosperity.
- The young woman who grew up in a critical home environment dreams of being a successful artist.
- The man who has been working at an unsatisfying job for ten years as the sole provider for his family dreams of starting his own business.

Whoever you are, whatever your dream is, I can guarantee that somewhere along the way, as you dare to dream and go for it, you will feel at least of few of these emotions:

- Fear
- Panic
- Anxiety
- Terror
- Doubt
- Disappointment
- Hopelessness
- Impatience
- Frustration
- Exasperation
- Anger

So, what do you do when this happens? Well, there are two answers. The first is the common trap into which many people fall. The second is the solution that will allow you to harness the power of your emotions.

The Trap

If your emotions are getting the better of you, you may have fallen into the common trap that snares many people who are in the beginning stages of accessing their power to create their own realities. When you feel the inevitable feelings that arise when pursuing your dreams, the trap is to think that it's *dangerous* to feel these feelings because you believe you will magnetize to you the very thing you *don't* want; or that you will *push away* your dream; or that you will be *counter-creating*. When this line of thinking arises, **your fear and resistance to these very natural thoughts and emotions will become a greater obstacle than the thoughts and emotions themselves.** Why? Because what you resist persists. In your resistance to these thoughts and feelings, you actually energize them with more and more energy and attention.

I can't tell you how many times I've heard clients struggle with, judge and resist their emotions in the pursuit of their dreams because they thought a book or teacher was telling them they should:

- Think away their fear.
- "Faith away" their anxiety.
- Just think positive.
- Get over it.
- Take a risk.
- Be proactive.

These techniques can work sometimes, and when they do, great. But when they don't, know that: a) your emotions are trying to tell you something, and b) there is an easier, gentler and more effective way to redirect the emotional energy that you are struggling with.

The Solution

The answer that solves all of the emotional challenges that will inevitably arise when pursuing your dreams allows you to take those very same emotions and use them productively and creatively. **When your emotions start percolating, the thing**

to do is CHOOSE TO FEEL. In order to exercise this choice, you must practice the following:
1. Accept and honor your feelings.
2. Allow them to release.
3. Listen for guidance.
4. Do as you are guided.

By embracing the discipline of these four steps, you will be well on your way to developing an empowering relationship with your emotions.

Emotions Are the Language of the Soul

Your soul is always communicating to you. It sends you a constant and continuous stream of guidance through the emotions you feel from moment to moment. And your soul is your conduit to all the answers to any questions you may have about how to have a fulfilling, fully expressed life. It sounds easy, but the challenge comes in that many people do not know how to interpret the messages our souls send us.

So, how do you access this oracle of wisdom? You do so by *allowing versus resisting* your emotions. Your soul is available 24/7 to guide you through your life. And the language your soul speaks is through the feelings you feel. Your soul does not communicate through your five senses. You do not see your soul with your eyes. You do not hear your soul with your ears. You do not taste your soul with your tongue. You do not feel your soul with your skin. And you do not smell your soul with your nose. But you sense your soul through your emotions.

- **When you feel bad,** it is your soul telling you that you're thinking thoughts (i.e., attracting to yourself) things that are contrary to what you (your highest you) truly wants.
- **When you feel good,** it is your soul telling you that you're thinking thoughts (i.e., attracting to yourself) things that you want (i.e., things that are aligned with your greatest, purest, most soul-based fulfilling desires).

This is how your soul guides you every moment of your life.

Metaphysics 202

Now, in order to manage the human tendency of having emotions, not only is it important to understand how allowing or resisting your emotions can serve or hinder you in the pursuit of your dreams, but it is also important to understand the connection between your emotions and Source Energy. And for that, we must take a little time out for another lesson in metaphysics. Remember when I told you that we are multidimensional beings? Well, we are going to revisit that concept from a slightly different angle so as to understand the process of manifestation in greater depth.

In the process of manifestation, we play with three dimensions: the 5th, the 4th and 3rd dimensions. There are many names for these three dimensions. In the model I use, the 5th dimension is the realm of the infinite, the 4th dimension refers to the conscious and subconscious realm of our psychology and the 3rd dimension refers to our third dimensional reality (that aspect of life that we interpret with our five senses). The concept of multiple dimensions is universal. Below* you will see the many ways this point is illustrated:

5th Dimension	4th Dimension	3rd Dimension
The Seed	The Soil	The Plant
The Father	The Holy Spirit	The Son
Source Energy	Creative Process	Result
God	Universal Law	Physical Manifestation
First Cause	Thoughts	Conditions
The Absolute	Beliefs	Experience
Divine Spirit	Imagination	Creation
Spirit	Mind	Body

The above analogies were compiled from various New Thought sources, including the works of Ernest Holmes.

For the sake of simplicity I'm going to use the terms *Soul consciousness (5ᵗʰ), personality consciousness (4ᵗʰ),* and *manifest consciousness (3ʳᵈ)* to explain how we play with these three dimensions.

Imagine that you could see ALL of you, not just the obvious physical part of you (your body), but different aspects of your consciousness as well. At the very core of your being is your

soul consciousness, shining love, joy, peace and wisdom in, as, and through you all the time. Around your soul is another layer of consciousness, which is your **personality conscious- ness**. Within this layer, you hold thoughts and emotions that are both conscious and unconscious. The emotions held within this personality layer include all of your emotions – everything from love, joy, gratitude, peace and harmony to anger, fear, sad- ness, guilt and conflict. The thoughts held in this layer include conscious and unconscious thoughts and beliefs about you, oth- ers, life, the world and the universe. The final layer is the **man- ifest consciousness**. This consciousness holds the concrete conditions of life – that which most people consider "reality." These conditions are not actually reality, but the end result of that which is true reality – life force – expressing through thoughts and emotions.

Now here is where the power of emotions begins to reveal itself. Imagine for a moment that these three layers of conscious- ness were a movie projector (soul consciousness), film (person- ality consciousness), and a movie screen (manifest consciousness). In much the same way that a projector shines a light through film to project an image onto a movie screen, our three levels of consciousness work together to create that which we experience as our reality. **Your soul consciousness – al- ways shining its loving light – shines through your per- sonality consciousness (your thoughts and emotions), infusing them with life-force energy, to create a mani- fested projection of those thoughts and emotions out in your "real world" experience.**

When the film has dark images (i.e., "negative" thoughts and emotions) on it, less light can shine through and the image we see on the screen is dark. When the images on the screen are more transparent ("positive" thoughts and emotions), the imag- es on the screen are more light-filled. In much the same way, when the thoughts and emotions you hold in your personality consciousness make you unhappy, then those are the things that are made manifest in your life. Conversely, when the thoughts and emotions you hold in your personality consciousness are ones that make you happy, then happy things are infused with the life-force energy and are made manifest in your life.

The trick to manifesting happy things is to find ways to feel happier more of the time. If you hold happy thoughts and emotions in your personality consciousness, they will be illuminated and magnetized, projected onto the screen of your life and drawn into your experience. If, on the other hand, you hold unhappy thoughts and emotions in your personality consciousness, they will be illuminated and magnetized, projected on the screen of your life and drawn into your experience.

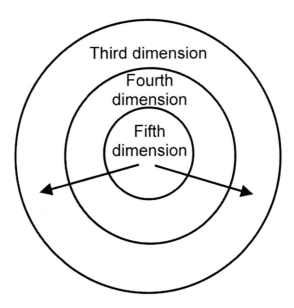

So, the big question becomes, **How do you keep your personality consciousness filled with happy thoughts and emotions and rid yourself of unhappy thoughts and emotions?** The answer is twofold:

- **Happiness is already inside you**. You don't need to get it, find it or catch it. It is already there. Your soul, connected to Source, is pumping you full of joy all the time, for you are an individualized expression of Source and Source is JOY. All you need to do is peel away the layers of resistance that keep you from experiencing the happiness. Since your soul consciousness is constantly radiating love, light, freedom, joy and peace, the only things preventing you from experiencing your true nature are the thoughts and emotions you hold in your personality consciousness.

· **You rid yourself of the unhappy thoughts and emotions by letting them go.** There are only two ways that unhappy thoughts and emotions stay in your personality consciousness. One scenario occurs when you give unhappy thoughts and emotions lots of energy, by consciously or unconsciously focusing on what you *don't* want vs. what you *do* want – ruminating over the bad things of the past, complaining to anyone who will listen, or sharing the same story over and over again about *that thing that happened to you*. All this energy causes you to keep manifesting more of your "feel bad" reality, because it is the film you've put in your projector. Source Energy does not judge what it illuminates in your life. It is consistent and impersonal, and it will manifest for you whatever you focus on.

The second way you keep "negative" energy formations in your personality consciousness is when you resist the negative thoughts and emotions. The resistance can be unconscious or conscious. Mentally, that resistance looks like an unchallenged limiting belief. And emotionally, that resistance looks like emotions you suppress, repress, push down, ignore, deny and otherwise keep trapped inside you. The unconscious thoughts and emotions may seem trickier to release because you don't even know they are there. But, when you practice allowing rather than resisting, it is amazing to see what can come to the surface. And, when necessary, you can get the help of a teacher, counselor or healer to help you identify the unconscious limitations you're holding within you. When you accept your emotions and honor them in constructive ways, *they will release*. And once the emotions release, amazing things start to happen. It is in *choosing to feel* that you begin to harness the power of your emotions.

The Journey

The catalyst that brought me to the threshold of my relation-ship with my own emotions was my struggle with compulsive eating and bulimia. I had been in therapy for about three years and had become very eloquent in my ability to articulate my issues. However, I rarely expressed any emotion. (I now affec-tionately refer to myself at that time as the "talking head.") I lived in my cerebral world, analyzing myself to death. I could find causes and effects for all my issues, but I experienced little relief in the form of healing. *To actually feel healed, to feel free … That eluded me.*

Well, one day, all of the stars aligned in my favor and I came across a class taught at the local adult education center called, *Developing a Healthy Relationship with Food and Your Body.* I signed up and discovered, much to my surprise, that my issues with food and body had little to do with food and body but had everything to do with my emotions. I learned I had no idea how to feel my feelings, much less understand why I should even bother engaging in such a useless, messy, out-of-control activi-ty. "This emotional stuff was all so irrational, illogical, manipu-lative and weak!"

I surrendered to the experience because, if there was one thing I knew, it was that what I *had* been doing wasn't working! Through the class, I began to discover an entire universe of di-vine intelligence, all accessible to me if I would only open the door to my emotions. Of course, I didn't feel this elation and ecstasy at the time. This became true only after several years of emotional growth and evolution. But, nonetheless, it was true. There really was something to these emotions. Emotions, it turned out, were much more than fodder for the quintessential therapist impersonation: "So, how does that make you FEEEEEEL?" I learned that my relationship with my emotions was all about my relationship with my self, and through the exploration of new ideas and doable techniques, I began a jour-ney of self-discovery and liberation.

This journey is not for the faint of heart. It takes courage. It takes the realization that what you've been doing up until now hasn't worked. And it often takes the support and guidance of mentors, teachers, healers and counselors. Many times, the denial of emotions goes hand in hand with disempowering behaviors. These behaviors can range from the mild emotion-avoidance techniques of excessive TV watching and sleep, to the self-destructive behaviors connected with addictions and compulsions, such as substance abuse, sex addiction and gambling, to name a few. What follows are exercises that can take you to *your* next step in harnessing the power of your emotions. Please know this book provides only a small piece of the bigger picture. If any part of you feels you need help, then give yourself the gift of getting the help you need. If you listen to your heart and gut, you will know.

The following discussion and exercises open you to the journey of developing an empowering relationship with your emotions. This section will teach you a four-step process that can ultimately lead to a new world of emotional freedom and empowerment. You will learn how to:

1. Discover and deconstruct the ideas you have about your emotions so as to discover what is really true for you.
2. Recognize when there are emotions to be honored.
3. Say 'yes' to emotions and accept them.
4. Become willing to honor your emotions, feel them and let them release.

When you practice these four steps, then the *power* of what emotions have to offer will reveal itself:

 • You feel lighter, freer, clearer.
 • You experience healing.
 • You become open to receiving guidance and insights from your soul.
 • You manifest more of what you desire.

What Happens When You Choose to Feel

When you honor and release your emotions, empowering things happen. First, **you feel better, lighter and freer.** This is the immediate effect and it holds true for all emotions. It is just as important to honor and release sadness, anger or fear as it is to honor joy, love and gratitude. People don't hold back just the "negative" emotions; they also hold back the "positive" ones.

The reason many people hold back emotions is that they think that it is the *emotions* that make them feel bad. This is a source of great misunderstanding. Granted, *yes*, emotions like grief, anger, sadness and fear are *not* fun to experience. They can really hurt! But the hurt *will release* when you honor the emotions, and then they will be gone until the next time you need to feel them.

What *really* makes people feel bad is *resisting* the feelings. You'll feel really bad when, instead of letting the feelings pass through you and release, you push them down, judge them, suppress them, repress them, eat them away, smoke them away, have sex them away, drug them away, shop them away ... any of the many ways we avoid our feelings. When you do this, the emotions stay inside you. They stay trapped in your personality consciousness and *that's* what you will consistently manifest in your life ... until you release them.

Another empowering thing that happens when you choose to feel is that **you receive insights**. Remember, your soul is offering you divine guidance all the time, but if you deny your emotions, you are denying the soul's method of communication. When you choose to feel, however, and let the emotions release, suddenly you'll be able to receive your soul's guidance. Answers will come to you that you were seeking before but couldn't find, no matter what you did or how hard you tried. These insights may come as inspiration, 'aha' moments or sudden clarity.

And yet another empowering thing that happens when you choose to feel is that **you manifest more and more of what you want**. When you begin to release the resistance that unexpressed emotions create and begin receiving insights, you'll start changing what you're holding in your personality consciousness. And as you do this, you're essentially putting in a different film to be projected on to the screen of your life. These more empowering thoughts and emotions allow more high-vibrational Source Energy through, to illuminate, magnetize and draw to you more of what you want in your life.

So, the way to harness the power of choosing to feel is as follows:
  · When you feel good, sustain your feeling and allow Source Energy to keep magnetizing your desires.

- When you feel bad, choose to feel and release your emotions so that they cannot block or hinder the free flow of Source Energy's magnetic attraction of your dreams.

The concept is simple; the journey, however, is deep and soulful. And now that you understand how and why it works, it's time to *get to* work. It is not necessarily easy to develop a healthy relationship with your emotions. However, when you strengthen your ability to manage this human tendency, you tap into unimaginable creative power in your life.

Exercise

Now, before you can get where you're going, you need to know where you are. So, before we delve into the tools that will help you to take your next steps in harnessing the power of your emotions, you'll need to first figure out exactly what kind of relationship you currently have with your emotions.

Below are a few questions for you to write about and reflect upon. Really give yourself time to explore these questions. Your answers will provide you with valuable insights on this journey of discovery. Once you feel complete with this exercise, continue on. Then we'll spend some time debunking the myths and discovering some truths about emotions.

- How do you feel about your emotions?
- What do you do with your emotions?
- Why do you do what you do with your emotions?
- What are your thoughts and beliefs about emotions?
- Where do your thoughts and beliefs come from?

The Tendency to Resist Feeling Our Feelings

Most people resist feeling their feelings ... at least to some degree. There are many ways we do this: We stop ourselves; we numb ourselves; we distract ourselves; we judge ourselves; we use logic and analysis in an attempt to solve our emotions as if they were problems; we rationalize, justify, or try to make sense of the way we feel. Sometimes we are aware of what we're doing, sometimes not.

People have all kinds of beliefs about emotions; beliefs that limit them in so many ways. Our relationship with our emotions is learned. We get messages about our emotions through verbal and nonverbal messages, as well as through the example of parents, significant adults and defining events in our lives. Below is a list of some of the beliefs and behaviors people have about emotions that keep them blocked:

- Emotions are bad.
- Men don't cry.
- Being emotional means I'm weak.
- I'm afraid of my emotions.
- If I feel my emotions they will never stop.
- If I feel my emotions I will die.
- If I feel my emotions I won't be able to function.
- Some emotions are good or ok, others are bad or unacceptable.
- "I'm not angry."
- "Don't be angry."
- "I'm not sad."
- "Don't be sad."
- "Don't cry."
- Emotions are problems to be solved.
- Emotions are irrational.
- I don't know how to feel my emotions.
- I'm stuck in my head.
- If I feel my emotions I will lose control.
- If I feel my emotions, I will hurt somebody.
- and the list goes on ...

Do any of these sound familiar? Can you add any more to the list based on what you've discovered about your own relationship with your emotions? What have you learned so far? This would be a good time to reflect and write some more.

The Emotional Spectrum

There is a spectrum in how you can relate to your emotions. On one end of the spectrum, you **control your emotions**. On the other end of the spectrum, **your emotions control you**. The place of balance and emotional power is where you **choose to feel.**

You Control Your Emotions	YOU CHOOSE TO FEEL	Your Emotions Control You

Looking at your relationship with your emotions in this way can help shed light on how it is possible to become the master of your emotions. If you're not the master of your emotions, then your emotions are your master and you fall at their mercy, sometimes consciously, many times not. When your emotions are your master, they become a limiting force in your life rather than the magic key that unlocks the answers you hold within. When you **choose to feel**, you honor your emotions. **To honor your emotions means to accept them, and give them permission and space to be felt and released.** When you honor your emotions, control is no longer part of the dynamic.

When You Control Your Emotions

Examples of what it can look and feel like when you're controlling your emotions include:

- Tension.
- Stress.
- Anxiety.
- Sleeplessness.
- What I call the "gerbil wheel syndrome," which means that instead of *feeling* and releasing your emotions, your mind goes into overdrive ruminating over circling thoughts, playing out scenarios, analyzing and "trying to figure things out logically."
- Resorting to unhealthy crutches such as overeating, smoking, overspending, substance abuse ...activities that distract you from your feelings. These distraction behaviors are often linked to compulsions or addictions.
- Wanting to sleep a lot.
- Procrastination.
- Feeling obsessed.

When Your Emotions Control You

Examples of what it can look and feel like when your emotions control you include:

- Being a "drama queen."
- Your personality takes on the expression of the emotion. For example, when someone's emotions control him, you might say, "He's an angry person." When that person, instead, chooses to feel, you might say, "He's feeling angry." When someone's emotions control her, you might say, "She is a lonely person." When that person, instead, chooses to feel, you might say, "She is feeling lonely."
- Your emotions cause you to do or say things you might regret (i.e., say things you don't mean, lash out, be hurtful, act impulsively, etc.)
- You may feel paralyzed in your ability to take action toward a goal.
- You may *appear* to be expressing emotions, but *not* feeling lighter or any release afterwards. Feeling as if you're still carrying around the emotion.
- You may "act out," which can be an unconscious behavioral release of emotion without the conscious awareness of the feeling.

Exercise

Write about and reflect upon the ways emotions might control you, and ways you control your emotions. Take the time to make an exhaustive list before you move on to the next section. Your answers will be very helpful as you practice choosing to feel. The behaviors you identify will become your own *personal red flags* from this point forward. These red flags will become your best friends. This is because, as you discover how to harness the power of your emotions, your red flags will catch your attention and say, "Hey, you're doing that thing again. Maybe there's an emotion you need to honor."

Choosing To Feel

In order to harness the power of your emotions, you must realize that you have a choice and that you are not at the mercy of
your emotions. You will need to understand and practice what
may be some new ideas and behaviors:

- If you've been denying your emotions, you will need to
  relearn when your soul is communicating to you. If the
  emotions are not readily accessible, there will be signals
  in your body and mind that tell you there is an emotion.

- At the moment you notice there is an emotion, *you have
  the choice to feel it*. If you choose to feel it, you accept it,
  and let it come up, come out and release.

- When you choose to feel, you embrace the emotion with
  complete love, and you release any and all judgment you
  may have around the emotion. You acknowledge that
  ALL emotions are completely okay, and that you get to
  feel the way you do, NO MATTER WHAT. You understand that your emotions are NOT you and that they are
  simply energy passing through your body that needs to
  be released so your soul can speak to you.

As you're able to consciously choose to feel more and more in
your life, and you have the experience of RELEASING your
emotions in healthy and productive ways, you will experience
many powerful things. You will begin to experience a sense of
healing in your life, which may have eluded you until now – the
kind of healing that comes when you finally release pain, sadness, fear and wounds you've been carrying around in your body
and psyche all this time. You will begin to gain insights and
find answers that you couldn't find before. You will begin to trust
yourself more and more as you experience the empowerment
that's possible by letting your soul communicate to you and realize that you DO know your truth. You will experience greater
well-being because you will find that NO crutch can come close
to making you feel as emotionally satisfied as honoring your
emotions does.

How to Do It

The first thing to know and always remember is that *there is no right way to honor your feelings.* I cannot emphasize this enough. As soon as you get caught up in doing this "right," you are already dishonoring, judging and controlling your feelings. So, right now, **let go of "doing this right."** Simply focus on discovering what *works* for you. Give yourself permission to be *free* to know what works for you around honoring and releasing your emotions.

That being said, I will offer you some techniques I've learned, experimented with and taught. Play around with them, experiment, combine them or try something new. Let this be your own personal discovery process in your relationship with yourself. You are nurturing your relationship with your soul.

Among the three techniques I am about to offer as a starting point, there are two common steps: 1) honoring the emotion, and 2) releasing the emotion. To honor something means to acknowledge and respect it. To release something means to let it go.

Recognizing an Emotion

In all three techniques, you begin by acknowledging there is (or might be) an emotion that needs to be released. This is where those red flags come into play. In the beginning of this journey, you'll simply want to practice *noticing* the red flags. And when you do, use your red flag mantra, "Hey, you're doing that thing again. Maybe there's an emotion you need to honor." That's all you need to do. This will be your way of beginning to say yes to your emotions.

You may still want or need to engage in your control-based behavior. **That's okay.** Remember, what you resist persists. If that behavior is *not critical,* like overeating, sleeping, watching TV, then you'll want to practice being as loving and accepting of yourself as possible. Say to yourself, "It's okay. I know I have a choice here. Right now I still want to choose this ice cream. I know I could choose to feel, too, but this is where I'm at." If your control-based behavior is critical, this is where you'll need to develop and/or practice an intervention technique. Critical behaviors are the ones that are imminently more destructive or dangerous, such as drinking if you've been abstinent or hitting if you've been violent. Saying, "It's okay," does **not** give you license to do these things. What you *are* saying is, "It's okay that you want to do this thing. It means there's some emotion here that needs to be honored." **In these situations, you need to have (or find if you have not yet) a support system to intervene on the critical behavior. This is where therapists, counselors, support groups and 12-Step programs can be life preservers.**

Once you've acknowledged there is an emotion (by recognizing a red flag or simply knowing), and that you have a choice, it's time to make your choice. You may feel ready to choose to feel. If so, then STOP, and move on to the section below called *The Feelings Process.*

If, however, upon recognizing the emotion, you choose the control-based behavior, you will notice afterward that the feeling that compelled you to engage in that behavior is still there. Furthermore, you may very well feel other feelings, such as remorse, regret or self-judgment. Here's where you get to break the cycle. Again, you practice more self-talk. Say to yourself, "You're learning. You're doing your best. It's okay. You still have a choice. Do you want to honor your emotions, NOW?"

What often happens here is that eventually you get to the place where you DO choose to feel because you understand how the control-based behavior isn't helping you. When you arrive at the place that you're ready to choose to feel, then you STOP what you're doing and move on to the next step, which is *The Feelings Process.*

The Feelings Process

If you've made the choice to feel, then you'll need to STOP and turn your attention within. Stop and give yourself the time and space to honor and release the emotion. (Now, I *do* know that this is not always practical or possible in the moment and further on, I'll explain how to honor and release your emotions when they come up at the most inopportune time.)

If feeling your feelings is a completely new concept, you may need to make an extra effort to create the time and space to feel. Some people need to remove themselves completely from where they are and find a space that feels safe and private. Some people need to connect with nature or light a candle. Some people need to listen to music that helps them connect with their heart. Do whatever works. Once you've acknowledged that there is a feeling and stopped to honor it, you can try one of the following techniques to honor and release the feelings:

The Exploration Method

With the exploration method, you'll want to sit quietly with your eyes closed and turn your attention within. As you do, bring your attention to where you might be holding an emotion in your body. Go to that place in your body and begin exploring what is there for you. You can do this by silently asking your body questions such as, "What do I need to know? What do you have to tell me?" You can do this by seeing if there is a word, an image or a sense of something. You can talk to your body and give it loving and accepting messages such as, "It's okay. I honor you. I'm listening. Go ahead and talk to me. I'm here for you."

If there is information there, explore it. See if the feeling or sensation wants to release. Sometimes release will come in the form of tears. Sometimes you'll need an activity or some help to release. You may be guided to speak out loud, write, scream into or hit a pillow, go for a walk, call a friend or do some artwork. Sometimes you'll feel like nothing's happening. Whatever your experience, **it's all okay**. Trust the process. See if your attention wants to go to another part of your body. Try exploring elsewhere in your body. When you feel like stopping, take a moment to tell yourself, "Thank you. I'm ready to honor you. Anytime. Let me know."

The Breath Method

With the breath method, you'll also want to sit quietly with your eyes closed and turn your attention within. With this technique, you will practice doing the *opposite* of the natural tendency with emotions. The tendency is usually to *push away* "negative feelings" because you simply don't want to feel bad. That's human nature. You want the feelings to go away. *With this technique, however, you practice accepting them with love using your breath.*

Whatever you're feeling, take a deep breath in and imagine you're breathing in – **taking in** – the feeling. Hold the breath for a beat. Then exhale love and acceptance. Then, again, take in the feeling with your inhale. Hold it. Exhale love and acceptance. Keep doing this until you feel complete. Many times, whatever you're feeling will begin to move and release in some way. Tears may flow. You may want to breathe with some kind of moaning noise. Trust yourself. Listen to your body. Allow the release to happen.

The Activity Method

With the activity method, you get physical. Many times, you'll feel emotions in your body in a very physical way. And you'll feel like you need to release the emotions physically. Go for a walk. Scream into a pillow or in a car with the windows rolled up. Pound a pillow. Go to the racquetball court or the batting cage. Whack some weeds with a hoe. Hit a punching bag. Whatever works for you, do it. The important thing is that you do this physical activity with *intention*. The intention is to honor and release the emotional energy. So, if you're angry at someone or something, allow yourself to put words silently or out loud, to the physical activity. Use curse words. **Mentally,** *let 'em have it.* Give yourself permission. If you know you're scared and angry, when you go for a walk say to yourself, "I'm scared. I'm angry. I'm scared. I'm angry." Pound it out into the dirt with each step. (If you're conscious of Mother Earth energy, mentally ask her to mulch the emotional energy and send it back into the atmosphere to be recycled.) Remember, it's important to be safe and responsible with whatever activity you choose. This is supposed to help you, not hurt you.

Giving Voice to Feelings

Sometimes we know what we are feeling and sometimes we don't. When we don't, it is helpful to start with the basics. There are four basic emotions and they are easy to remember because three of them rhyme: *mad, glad, sad and scared.* Almost every emotion that exists is a variation of these four basic emotions. And when you're striving to honor your emotions, it can be really helpful to simply name them and mentally say "yes" to them. Even if you do not use any of the three techniques above, giving yourself permission and giving voice to your emotions is a powerful step. Also complementing the three techniques with words or voice can really help to get the emotional energy moving and releasing.

When Your Emotions Release

Just as you learn how to recognize when there is a feeling to be felt, you will also learn to recognize when you have released emotional energy. You'll feel it physically, mentally and emotionally. You may feel lighter. You may feel less turmoil or tension inside. You may feel as if something in you has let go. You may feel as if you can breathe again. You may feel tired and the need to sleep. You may feel calmer. You may feel one emotion release and a different one rise up. As you practice honoring and releasing your emotions, practice recognizing how it feels when they have released.

When you begin to release emotions, an energetic shift happens within you. When you release emotions, you're also releasing resistance. And when resistance is released, your soul can more easily communicate to you. This is the time to listen.

Listening For Guidance

Listening for your soul's guidance is simply a matter of being open and receptive. Sometimes, when you release emotional energy, you will have an almost immediate insight or realization. You may suddenly find yourself seeing the source of your upset in a new light. You may feel as if you know what your next step is. You may receive an answer you were seeking. Sometimes the guidance comes later, when you least expect it. You release your emotional energy. You feel lighter. You go on with your life and then, poof, something comes to you.

Just like recognizing your red flags and recognizing release, you'll want to practice recognizing when your soul speaks to you. Remember, the soul does not communicate to you through your five senses; it communicates through emotions and feeling. So, if you've been a pretty analytical and logical person up until now, it may take some practice and willingness to recognize this new form of intelligence expressing within you. All it takes is willingness. The rest will happen.

And once you begin to listen, you'll have the opportunity to not only receive guidance, but also to act upon it. At first, you may not completely trust what your soul is telling you to do. So, you may listen with an, "Isn't that interesting?" ear and leave it at that. If you stay open and receptive, your soul's nudges may get louder and less easy to dismiss. Eventually, you may feel ready to act on the inner nudges.

The first inspired actions may feel risky, but as you keep taking the risks, you will likely discover that your soul's guidance is worth trusting. You may go through periods where you confuse your soul's guidance for some other internal voices – the voice of your parents, the voice of society, the voice of your fears, the voice of "the shoulds." As you practice honoring your emotions, you will get better and better at distinguishing the voice of your soul's guidance versus the other voices that float around in your mind.

Exercise

The following exercise is designed to help you become more aware of your emotional energy. Through this exercise, you'll begin to notice the types of behaviors and situations that can be related to unreleased emotions. Remember, unreleased emotions can keep you stuck in any number of ways in your life.

Review the list below, checking off anything you have experienced in your life on a regular basis. You may be unfamiliar with what some of these things mean. If you don't know what something means but it somehow "resonates" for you, or you've heard people use these terms, ask someone you trust about it. You may discover that you engage in the behavior or have had the experience, but didn't realize it.

- Nervous talking
- Nervous laughing
- Inability/discomfort/fear of being alone with no distractions
- Tension
- Stress
- Anxiety
- Sleeplessness
- The "gerbil wheel syndrome," which means that instead of FEELING and releasing your emotions, your mind goes into overdrive, possibly obsessing, ruminating over circling thoughts, playing out scenarios, analyzing or "trying to figure it out logically." In other words, your mind keeps running on the gerbil wheel, but you're not getting anywhere.
- Resorting to unhealthy crutches, such as overeating, smoking, overspending, substance abuse – generally things that can be linked with compulsive or addictive behaviors.
- Wanting to sleep a lot
- Procrastination
- Being a "drama queen"
- Your personality takes on the expression of the emotion OR you BECOME the emotion. For example, you may have heard someone say something like, "You're an angry person." "She's a lonely person." (In contrast, when you're feeling and releasing the emotion, you would instead hear something like, "You are FEELING angry." "She is feeling lonely.")
- Your emotions cause you to do things that you might regret (i.e., say things you don't mean, lash out, be hurtful, act impulsively, etc.)
- You might feel paralyzed in your ability to take action toward a goal.

- You appear as if you are expressing emotions, but you do NOT feel any lighter or any release afterwards. You feel like you are still carrying around the emotion.
- You "act out."

Now that you've checked off the scenarios that seem relevant to you, write about any or all of these experiences. Explore the things going on in your life *before* these behaviors arise for you. In other words, what are the triggers for these behaviors or experiences?

Also, notice if any of these scenarios *describe* you. If they do, they may be some of your personal red flags. You may want to make a short list of your red flags. The more aware of them you are, the easier it will be to notice them and use them to alert you to the possibility that you have some feelings you may want to honor.

More Things to Know About Emotions

Harnessing the power of your emotions is a rich opportunity. There is much to know. The following section offers more insight into how we resist our emotions and what a healthy and productive relationship with our emotions looks like.

Holding Back Positive Emotions

It is helpful to understand that we not only resist "negative" emotions, but we also resist "positive" emotions. This happens for many reasons. Oftentimes, we will not let ourselves be happy, free, joyful or enthusiastic because, when we were in the past, we experienced negative consequences. Maybe as a child, you got negative feedback whenever you were joyful, free and enthusiastic, or your bubble was burst one too many times. Sometimes we won't allow ourselves to feel content because of a limiting belief. You may think that a dream will be dashed, "It's too good to be true," or something bad will eventually happen, so why bother getting your hopes up. It is important to acknowledge *all* the ways you resist emotions, no matter what they are, because resistance is resistance, and if you're holding back any emotions, you will not be able to harness their power. The resistance of "positive" emotions usually means there are "negative" emotions or thoughts beneath them, and it is *that* energetic structure that will hold the status quo in your personality consciousness, manifesting *that* reality until you honor and release it.

You'll Never Get More Than You Can Handle

As I said before, the journey of developing a healthy and productive relationship with your emotions is not for the faint of heart. It does take courage and oftentimes support. You may have to confront fears and a level of emotional intensity that will likely feel unfamiliar and unsafe to you. For this reason, at times the emotional energy you experience may seem overwhelming.

In support of this challenging opportunity, a well-known quote, reported to have come from Mother Teresa, can offer some solace and humor, "I know God will never let me have more than I can handle. I just wish He didn't trust me with so much." There is great truth in this. Although you may feel overwhelmed at times on your emotional journey, you will never get more than you can handle. You will probably get more than you'd like, but not more than you can handle.

Now, it would be irresponsible to use the word "never" without a bit of clarification. Yes, there are people and situations where emotional trauma is so extreme, that it is indeed more than a person can handle. There are certain personality types and forms of abuse and tragedy that can be associated with mental illness. But it's important to put this fact into perspective and understand that the vast majority of people can, with the right support and understanding, handle even extreme emotional intensity. If this were not the case, there would be a lot more non-functioning people walking around in the world. On the flip side, if you want proof of how much the human spirit can handle, you don't have to look very far. There are endless examples of people who have suffered great loss and tragedy, who have not only withstood it but risen to such great heights of love, compassion and courage that it boggles the mind. Sometimes, you just don't know what you're made of until you decide that you are willing to find out. And choosing to honor your emotions can provide just one such opportunity.

Our minds have amazing ways of protecting us, and we have self-preservation built into our psyches. Even some forms of mental illness, such as multiple personalities, are ways the mind protects itself from trauma. And so, for the vast majority, we will not allow ourselves to open up to more than we are ready for at any time. As our will allows, we will open up to just enough to have to stretch and grow. And if you are willing and intentional about the journey, you will allow into your life the support you need. Courage, support and gentleness are key.

Inopportune Moments for Emotions

Once you've decided you're willing to travel this journey of learning how to honor your emotions, you may encounter the common experience of having emotions rising to the surface at the most inopportune times. Maybe you're at work and there's simply no space for you to feel your feelings. Or you are with people and simply can not get away. When this happens, you can practice *deferring* honoring your emotions for a better time and space.

When you notice the feelings coming up, rather than simply suppressing them and moving on with life, take a few seconds to practice a bit of self-talk. Say to yourself, "I feel you. I know you are there. I'll honor you later." And then take a few deep breaths and do what you have to do. A simple acknowledgment that there are feelings can do wonders for honoring your emotions and helping you to manage them in the moment. Then make sure that as soon as you can, hopefully within the same day, you give yourself the opportunity to choose to feel. It may seem trickier to get back in touch with the feelings but usually it isn't as hard as you might think. Unexpressed emotions don't just go away. They simply get parked in your personality consciousness. And once you've opened the door to letting your emotions become a conscious part of your life, they are usually pretty accessible. It may simply require the use of some feelings process techniques to prime the pump.

When the Feelings Won't Flow

There will be times when you can tell there are feelings to be felt, but you just can't seem to access them. You might feel a low-grade depression and that there is some emotion underneath but you can't seem to get at it. You may know you are sad and need a good cry, but the tears won't flow. You might feel anxious or agitated, but can't identify the source. Your vices or crutches may feel as if they've taken on a life of their own and your red flags are waving wildly, but you're just not in a place to choose to feel.

When this happens, it is important, once again, to practice allowing versus resistance. Simply allow yourself to be where you're at. This is a time to practice self-talk. Give yourself messages of love and acceptance. Also, take time to clarify your willingness and intention to honor your emotions. Some examples of self-talk may sound like:

- Yep, you're depressed right now and can't seem to shift it and that's okay.
- Yes, I seem to be stuck in my late night compulsive TV eating right now, and I'm still willing to feel my feelings and move out of this place.
- I'm just down right now and nothing's coming up. I'm going to let myself be where I am.

It's virtually impossible to shift your emotional energy if you resist and judge yourself for where you are. Once you've tapped into the energy of allowing, then you can listen for guidance as to what actions you might want to take to move beyond the stuckness. Usually, all it takes is doing *anything* different than what you are currently doing, simply because anything different is just that – *different*. And once your attention is focused on something else, your vibration shifts and movement can happen.

Call a friend, go for a walk, turn off the TV, just go into your backyard or take a shower. Less is more here. When you are down and feeling stuck, it can be very hard to get motivated to do anything so pick something small. One small step toward anything different can get the ball rolling in a different direction. And once you're moving in a different direction, you can listen for more guidance as to what you might need to honor your emotions.

Mixed Emotions

One of the amazing things about emotions is that you can feel a whole bunch of seemingly contradictory emotions simultaneously. It is important to understand this and allow it to be. A common form of emotional resistance is to analyze or judge oneself for what you're feeling. **Emotions are not problems to be solved. They are energy to be allowed (felt and released).** And all emotions are okay.

Sometimes, it takes great honesty and permission to let yourself dare to feel what you feel. Often, all sorts of judgments and taboos come from family and society that would have us resist discovering the truth of how we feel. There are many life challenges that bring up big emotions and, if you can't find a way to allow them, they will remain stuck. Examples of this include the new mother who is supposed to be overjoyed with her new baby but feels overwhelmingly stressed, depressed and lonely. The man who needs to grieve the love he never got from his alcoholic mother in order to heal, but can't because he believes *men don't cry*. The sister who needs to honor the rage of feeling abandoned by the older brother who died, but who can't because she can't let herself be angry at her brother when she feels she should only hold him in loving memory.

Many, if not most of life's challenges, are emotionally complex. More times than not, you will feel several emotions simultaneously – sadness and relief, rage and love, fear and excitement, depression and anger. The more you practice holding a space for all of your emotions, the better you will become at honoring them. The release may come in waves, or what feels like layers that peel away to reveal underlying layers. Or the feelings might release as one blended emotional release. You don't have to name them. You don't even have to know what you're feeling. You can simply allow yourself to be emotional and honor whatever is there. The best way to practice allowing with mixed emotions is to simply *let them be.*

Factors That Influence Emotions

Many factors can influence your emotional state, in both positive and negative ways – body chemistry, nutrition, medication, exercise, alternative healing modalities, the environment, etc. As you develop a healthy and productive relationship with your emotions, you will become more self-aware on many levels. Not only will you become more conscious of what's going on for you mentally, emotionally and spiritually, but also you will likely become more tuned into your physical body as well. This heightened awareness is an important skill for harnessing the power of your emotions.

You may discover how much better you feel emotionally when you eat right and exercise. Or you may notice how irritable you feel when you take allergy medicine. You may find you hate the world before your menstrual period. Or that certain prescription drugs make you anxious. The key here is to simply be aware and notice, and take it all into consideration as you develop a healthy relationship with your emotions. If you find that external factors are influencing your emotional health, allow yourself to explore other options. There are many out there – traditional and nontraditional – and you never know which one has the capacity to make a positive impact on your mental and emotional health.

Trusting the Process

By now you've gathered that there is great power in your emotions, and that in understanding how to relate to them, you can harness their power. You've been offered numerous tools and techniques for practice and exploration. And now you are on your way. Each person's journey with their emotions is unique, and what works for one person might not work for another. As you travel this journey, remember, there is no right answer, just **your** answer. Trust the process. Trust your heart and trust your gut. There is great intelligence there that transcends any intelligence your cerebral mind may have to offer. If you stay open, willing and receptive on this journey, you will attract exactly what you need along the way and you will have the opportunity to tap into a source of wisdom, guidance and creative energy you may have never before known.

The Big Picture

As you embark or continue on your journey of making your dreams come true, you will go through many different stages: identifying your dream, getting clarity, setting goals, identifying action steps, developing a strategy, taking risks, getting stuck, failing, trying again, succeeding, reevaluating, redefining your dream, etc.

Through this process, you may feel *lots of emotions*, which can include, but are not limited to, fear, numbness, excitement, anticipation, anger, frustration, hope, hopelessness, apathy, boredom, disillusionment, awe and fulfillment.

When you understand that these kinds of emotions are all part of the journey, you will not stop when they show up. You will simply recognize the emotions as part of the process and say to yourself, "Oh, there you are, I was expecting you. Now that you're here, let's just honor you so you can come up, come out and release. That way, I can reap the benefit of whatever you have to give me on this wonderful adventure."

Many people misinterpret the difficult emotions that arise as a sort of Grim Reaper, coming to take their dreams away. His bony hand rises to decree, "YOU! You don't get to have this. You are doomed to a life of mediocrity and disappointment!" WRONG. These emotions are actually little angels that, because we've kept them in the dark, condemned to the dungeons of our belief systems, look like and feel like powerful demons. But, once you turn on the light and let them come up, come out and release, they lose all their power. To harness the power of your emotions is to use your emotions as doorways to the next piece of information you need. That's all they are! And when you effectively integrate your emotions into a new way of living life, then feelings such as fear, frustration, hopelessness, boredom, disillusionment, numbness and anger become the magic portals to the answers you seek.

Managing the Human Tendency of Emotions

Now that you understand how to harness the power of your emotions, it's time to get back to the nuts and bolts of managing this particular tendency so that you can continue to practice

Step III of The Formula and step out of your own way when your emotions do their thing. **To manage the human tendency of emotions means taking charge of your emotions rather than letting them take charge of you.** In order to do this, you must realize that emotions are not just something that happens to you, but they are actually a navigational tool for your life.

You can't help but be a creative being. You are creating all the time, whether you like it or not, with each thought you have. The Law of Attraction is at work whether or not you believe in it, whether or not you are conscious of it, and under all conditions.

Your Emotional Navigational System

As you go through your day, creating with your thoughts, your soul provides a steady stream of guidance through your emotions. All you need to do to continue manifesting what you desire, vs. what you do not desire, is to pay attention to your emotional energy. As you tune in more and more to your feelings, using them as your navigational system, not only will you feel better more and more of the time, but also you will be actively taking greater charge of creating the life of your dreams. Your emotions are your compass, your traffic signals, your map and your tour book, all rolled in to one. When you become skilled at using these tools, you can reach any dream destination you could ever imagine.

Your Emotional Traffic Light

The first level of communication is like your traffic light telling you to stop or go:
- When you feel good, that's your green light telling you to keep doing what you are doing. You are being you fully expressed. You are living your truth.
- When you feel bad, that's your red light, telling you to stop, pay attention and look at your map.

Your Emotional Map

The second level of communication occurs when you actually stop to pay attention. When you feel bad, that's your soul telling you you're putting forth creative energy (your thoughts) that is contrary to what you truly want. In other words, you've lost your way. Your awareness and your emotions, like a map, will tell you where to go.

When You Get Lost

There are three "bad neighborhoods" where you can get lost in negative thoughts and emotions that are counterproductive to what you are trying to create in your life. These neighborhoods are located in the Bad Habit, the Gerbil Wheel, and the Magnetic Whirlpool districts. If you get lost in any of these neighborhoods, your built-in navigational system should put you back on the right path quite easily.

The Bad Habit District

A common bad habit one can easily fall prey to is the bad habit of focusing on what you don't want. If you find yourself feeling bad because your attention is focused on the wrong thing, then you can often shift your energy simply by exercising your choice to focus on what you want vs. what you don't want. It can take seconds to minutes to completely shift your awareness to a more productive flow of emotional energy.

The Gerbil Wheel District

The gerbil wheel refers to the feeling you get in your head when your mind circles around and around over the same thoughts, scenarios or limiting beliefs. This can mean that your thoughts on a particular subject have been held for so long, energized by lots of emotion, that they have a life of their own. It can also be a well-ingrained avoidance mechanism that protects you from feeling emotions you don't know how or want to deal with. When you feel bad because you are caught on the gerbil wheel, there are two ways to get off: *the mental approach* and *the emotional approach.*

The mental approach to jumping off the gerbil wheel is to logically look at the thoughts and beliefs running the gerbil wheel. Your task is to find enough logical evidence to render the belief invalid. You can dismantle the thoughts and beliefs by identifying them, exploring them and challenging their basis. (The next chapter addresses limiting beliefs in depth.)

However, limiting beliefs are often held in place with emotions. The emotions are what give the beliefs life and keep the gerbil wheel in your head going. When this is the case, the solution is to *choose to feel* (the emotional approach). When your map points in this direction, it means you must choose to get out of your head and into your heart. It means you need to be willing to *feel* the pain, fear or sadness that these limiting beliefs cause you. When you go through the process of honoring and releasing, guidance often comes in the form of new insights and new beliefs that are based in a higher truth for you.

The Magnetic Whirlpool District

Sometimes when you feel bad, it's simply because you've had your attention focused on the *feel bad issue* long enough that the Law of Attraction has drawn to you enough feel-bad energy for you to be caught in a whirlpool of feeling bad. One solution is to exercise your choice to *focus on anything that feels good*. It may be hard at first – like the initial stretch and reach out of the whirlpool to *pull* yourself out of the vortex. But with steadfast commitment and intention, it is possible to get yourself out. You can leave behind the resistance of feeling bad, and soon enough, the feel good thoughts will have you walking on dry, happy land again.

If this doesn't work, you may need to use a different strategy with the whirlpool. In this situation, your map is pointing you to go deeper with your emotions. When you honor your emotions, you must be willing to release resistance and go into them. If you're not used to doing this, it can feel scary and unnatural. But the truth is, when you finally go into the emotions, they will come up, come out and release ... and you will be released, too. So, rather than pulling yourself out of the whirlpool, you may need to take a deep breath, let go of fighting the whirlpool, and let yourself be pulled underwater for a while. When you stop fighting the whirlpool, its force can now work in your favor, and you will be thrust up into the air, light and free.

Staying Out of Your Own Way

In order to successfully practice Step III of The Mystic's Formula, you will need to remain awake and aware regarding your emotions. If you are new to this level of mindfulness, it will require effort and discipline at first. You may find yourself falling into unconscious habits of emotional reactivity, getting lost in the neighborhoods of the Bad Habit of focusing on what you don't want, the Gerbil Wheel of limiting thoughts and beliefs, and the Magnetic Whirlpool of feeling bad. However, with practice, you will become more and more aware. The techniques outlined here will become easier and easier to use. And eventually, using your emotional navigational system will become second nature. You'll become highly attuned to your emotional state at any given moment, and you'll easily check in with yourself, shifting your energy by choosing to redirect your attention, and/or honoring your emotions as needed to release resistance. When you reach this level of easy communication with your inner wisdom, then you will have truly begun to tap into success for the soul.

17

Dismantling Limiting Belief Systems

"Once in a while it really hits people
that they don't have to experience the world
in the way they have been told to."

— *Alan Keightley*
author

Finding something positive, anything positive, about a situation that you struggle with can be challenging at times. You may deeply desire a fulfilling relationship, but nothing in your experience or history gives you any hope that it's possible. You may want to create financial abundance doing spiritually fulfilling work, but you are utterly convinced that higher purpose work and financial freedom are mutually exclusive, and you have all sorts of evidence to back up this belief. You may want to quit smoking and create a healthier lifestyle, but your history with failure and all your unhealthy friends make it feel impossible.

When you have a dream or goal that feels hopeless, you must first be willing to want "the impossible." Remember your *wanting mechanism?* (For a refresher, refer to *Obstacles to Identifying What You Want in* Step I.) Once you're willing to want what you want, no matter how impossible it may seem at first, then you must begin facing and confronting your beliefs about the dream. Beliefs are simply thoughts you've held for a long time and they are often kept in place because: a) you've never really challenged them, and b) there is emotional energy, often fear or past pain, that keeps giving those thoughts lots of life, and therefore lots of power, and therefore lots of magnetic energy to keep attracting more similar thoughts.

Scarcity, Limitation and Conditionality

Your beliefs become *limiting beliefs* when you believe in scarcity, limitation and conditionality. To believe in scarcity means to believe there is not enough – not enough love, not enough good, not enough forgiveness, not enough money, not enough time, etc. – simply *not enough*. This scarcity consciousness can apply to anything and everything. When you believe in limitation, it means you believe in the apparent finality of our third-dimensional world. You've bought into the idea that reality is what you can assess with your five senses. And you've adopted human judgments and perceptions as truth. Limitation can also be projected onto anything – God, people, situations, etc. When you believe in conditions, you've bought into erroneous cause-and-effect thinking. There *is* cause and effect in the Universe, but it becomes limiting when you get your cause and effect all wrong. Erroneous cause-and-effect thinking sounds like: "When I have a nice car, women will want me," "When I make more money, then my financial problems will go away," or, "When I lose weight, then I'll love myself."

The *only* cause in the Universe is *consciousness*. And your consciousness is the vibrational sum total of your thoughts, words and actions. If you believe women don't want you, they won't, nice car or not, until you change that belief. If you believe in your financial problems, money or not, they will not go away until you shift your consciousness. If you do not love yourself, no matter how much you weigh, that will not change until you think and feel lovingly toward yourself.

Dismantling Belief Systems

There are a number of effective ways to begin facing and dismantling your belief systems. One simple yet powerful way is to journal. Begin by owning your dream, no matter how impossible it may seem, and start asking yourself what your beliefs and feelings are regarding this particular dream. The following list of questions can help get you started:

- What would happen if this dream came true?
- What do I think that would mean for me, for others, for my life?
- What would happen if this dream didn't come true?
- What would that say about me?
- Why do I think this dream can not happen for me?
- Why do I think this dream is impossible?
- What would I have to let go of for this dream to become a reality?
- What sacrifice(s) would I have to make for this dream to become a reality?
- How might I need to grow for this dream to become a reality?
- What would I have to be willing to do for this dream to become a reality?

The answers to these questions will reveal a great deal, including the general thinking you maintain about this topic and hence, your consciousness of it.

Exercise

The Mental Purge

Another highly effective method for identifying and dismantling limiting beliefs is through the Mental Purge exercise. This process will allow you to bring up and out limiting beliefs that have kept you stuck. If you give yourself completely to this process and do not quit on it, you will absolutely begin to experience breakthroughs that will help you take back your power from your limiting beliefs. I use it regularly as part of the Vision Workshop and it really works.

To proceed, it's best to read the exercise once through first. Then set aside about two hours of uninterrupted time. Get out some lined paper. Two sheets, side by side, will form your worksheet. You'll use 1 – 3 worksheets, so make them ahead of time. Divide each page into two columns, so that when placed side by side, you have four columns total. Starting from the left, title each column as follows: A) The Reason It's Not Happening, B) Underlying Fear, C) Underlying Belief, D) Positive Truth. Now, somewhere at the top of your worksheet write down your dream. (e.g., "My dream of changing careers, My dream of being financially free, My dream of healing my body, My dream of getting married, or, My dream of traveling around the world for a year.")

Your worksheet will look like this:

A) Reason It's Not Happening	B) Underlying Fear	C) Underlying Belief	D) Positive Truth
1.			
2.			
3.			
4.			
5.			
6.			
7.			
8.			
9.			

Through this exercise, your dream will be your focus. You will be discovering, purging and dismantling the limiting beliefs that have prevented you from successfully pursuing your dream. Now you're ready to start.

Begin by filling in the worksheet one column at a time. Do not skip ahead.

1. First complete column A. PURGE yourself of *every reason* you can imagine why your dream is not happening yet. This is your opportunity to dump, vomit and expel every last reason, excuse, belief and thought you've ever had or could ever imagine that stops you from having this dream come true. Write down one reason per line. Use as many worksheets as necessary to ensure you leave no stone unturned before you move on to step 2.

2. Once you've completed column A, move on to column B. For *each and every reason* you listed, write down the underlying fear. For each fear, write in the following manner: "I am afraid that _____," or," I fear that _____." The reason for this is that this is not just a mental purge, but an emotional purge, as well. In order to dismantle

the limiting beliefs, you'll need to begin shifting the fear that keeps them in place. And the way to move fear is to honor it by owning it and allowing it. Repeating over and over again, "I'm afraid that _____," "I'm afraid that_____," or, "I'm afraid that_____" will allow you to face your fears and begin releasing them.

I promise you there will be a fear under each reason. And here is where it starts to get interesting. At some point in this exercise, and for some it begins here, people start to see repetition. It gets even more obvious when you move on to column C. This is due to the fact that there usually aren't a million reasons why people are stuck. There are usually only one or a very few. And these reasons, fears and beliefs disguise themselves and express themselves in a multitude of ways – virtually infecting your life. Once you realize you're only dealing with a handful of barriers, you're able to focus on the real issues (not the symptoms) to move forward.

3. Once you've completed column B, repetition and all, move on to column C and begin writing the underlying belief for each fear and reason. Yes, you need to list the underlying belief for *each and every fear*. Write it as follows: "I believe that _____." Sometimes people get stuck here, which is why having a buddy can be helpful. If you get stuck, skip that item and come back to it. Or, see if you can go deeper with the fear. Usually under a fear is another fear, and another. When you go deeper, sometimes a hard-to-identify belief reveals itself.

At about this time, people start to experience breakthroughs. First, people notice repetition. They see again there are not a million limiting beliefs but just one or a few that have controlled them throughout their lives. They see these beliefs are the fundamental lenses through which they see themselves and the world. Secondly, as they con-

tinue in the process, giggles, snickers, aha's and sighs of relief will inevitably percolate to the surface. People realize that the beliefs in which they have invested so dearly *are simply not true.* This is when people begin to feel their limiting beliefs breaking down and becoming dismantled.

4. Finally, when you have completed every last item in column C, move on to column D. And for each limiting belief write down a positive truth. This is a powerful column. **The purpose of column D is to identify the mantra you will use from this day forward as an antidote every time a limiting thought or fear surfaces as you pursue your dream.** It may be extra helpful in completing this column to reread the section on affirmations in Chapter 10. To complete the exercise, you will need to come up with a positive truth or affirmation regarding *each line* of reasoning, fearing and believing that has kept your dream at bay. You may discover that the only positive statements you can *really* buy into are the *statements of willingness* or *if/then statements.* You may also discover that, as you've distilled all your barriers to discover only a handful of limiting beliefs, you really only need one or two positive truths to keep you focused on your dream instead of your obstacle. Remember: the important thing about positive truths and affirmations is that you have to *really buy into them.* In other words, you need to find a positive statement that you believe, one that is true for you. If you are creating an affirmation that you don't believe, it just won't work.

Once you have completed the Mental Purge, you may feel tired or revitalized. This exercise has the power to shift your energy and consciousness in profound ways. It will give you tools to move toward your dream where you may have been blocked before.

Staying Out of Your Own Way

In order to successfully practice Step III of the Mystic's Formula you must use your inner witness to remain alert to any beliefs that may limit what you will allow in to your life. It all begins with willingness, awareness and practice. As you question your own cause and effect thinking and recognize thoughts of scarcity and conditionality, you will become more skilled at redirecting your attention toward positive truths. Manage your limiting beliefs and watch infinite possibilities reveal themselves!

18

Letting Go of Attachment

"The harder you fight to hold on to specific assumptions, the more likely there's gold in letting go of them."

— *John Seely Brown*
American scholar, scientist, Industry Hall of Fame inductee

John's level of stress escalated with each phone call. Over the past four months, bank after bank denied his loan applications. He was beyond tense. There was so much at stake; he had sold his house, moved his family to another state, and spent his life savings, all in pursuit of his dream business and lifestyle opportunity. For six months, he had done his homework, leaving no stone unturned, getting his ducks all lined up to take the big plunge. This big dream, the one he had dared to dream, was actually coming true. Then ... everything fell apart.

Upon arriving in what was to be their new home state to begin a new dream life, the storm began. The mortgage and business loans needed to close the deal fell through. Loan brokers revealed themselves to be unethical. Real estate agents revealed themselves to be incompetent. Harassing phone calls from the seller's lawyer became commonplace. John and his family were essentially homeless because their new home was tied into the new business. Living out of a hotel, the family's stress was compounded as they were in a new place without their usual support system. Their small children were getting sick without the benefit of a familiar family doctor or insurance. Extended family and friend issues boiled to the surface because financial promises, dependent on the close of the deal, were breaking as things fell apart. How could this be happening? John had done everything right. It felt like a nightmare from which he couldn't wake.

John needed a loan. And he needed it now. If he could just replace the loan that had fallen through, all their problems would be solved ... or so they thought. John and his wife became desperately attached to each new loan they applied for. *They made a loan the source of their peace.* Each hungry new loan officer made promises that the loan would be a piece of cake because John and his wife looked great on paper. *Each time, John became attached to that loan,* his hopes fueled by the loan officer's enthusiasm. But denial after denial, the banks decided the risk was too great and John realized that things were not as they seemed. He was getting desperate. He needed a loan to come through. The potential loss of his dream started to pale compared to the hardship he feared his family faced if everything fell through and they had to start all over with no home, no job, no plan and no friends.

Fortunately, John had a strong relationship with his wife, and enough of a relationship with Source, to navigate their way through the storm. Together they managed all the human tendencies, instincts and states of consciousness that arose – one at a time, a day at a time. They managed their egos, opening up to higher guidance when they felt separate from Source. They harnessed the power of their emotions by honoring them and allowing release, relief and inspiration in. They managed their limiting beliefs with a willingness to see a higher truth. And when their attachment to the loans consumed them, after months of desperately clinging to a loan as the solution to their problems, they eventually were able to let go ... to really let go. They finally arrived at a deep place of knowing that if a loan did not come through, it was not meant to be. For a loan was not their Source; only the Infinite One Within was their Source.

The Vibration of Separation

This story illustrates some of the very common challenges of attachment. We become attached to something when we believe that a person, thing, or condition is our source – the source of our love, our happiness, our serenity or our safety. **The problem, however, is that when you make something outside yourself your source, you are holding a consciousness and vibration of *separation*.** Remember, if you hold a consciousness of *having* or *being one* with something, you attract the same – *having* and *being one* with that thing. If, however, you become attached to something outside yourself, you are maintaining a vibration that the object of your desire is *separate* from you. As a result you attract the same – *being separate* from that thing.

Slamming the Door in the Universe's Face

Beyond the consciousness of separation, attachment presents yet another obstacle in the pursuit of your dreams. When you are attached to a particular thing you have decided is **the** answer, you have essentially slammed the door shut in the Universe's face! The Universe is infinitely abundant. It is constantly offering you **more** than you could ever need, want or desire. But, by Law of Attraction, if you say "I want a loan," you will allow only a loan into your life, even if the Universe is trying to give you a lottery win. If, however, you let go of the loan and allow the Universe to guide you to the answer which is for the highest and greatest good of all concerned, then you open up to receiving solutions you never imagined.

It's as if you were living in a cave on an isolated island, subsisting on the rice you were able to salvage from the ship. You see you're down to the last morsel and anxiously begin running from salvaged crate to salvaged crate, panicking, "I need more rice. I need more rice! There must be more rice in one of these crates. I know there was more rice. I'll die without rice." You become so consumed with finding rice that you're unable to see or allow anything else into your experience. You can't see that it's raining tropical fruit outside your cave and that the ground is covered with coconuts.

Managing Attachment

Your ability to manage attachment is directly related to your ability to manage the other three human tendencies, instincts and states of consciousness – your ego, your emotions and your limiting beliefs. For simplicity's sake, let's call them the *three amigos*. If the three amigos are running the show, your consciousness is vibrating somewhere in the vicinity of separation (the ego), fear (emotions), and scarcity (limiting beliefs). These three almost always lead to the compulsion to control things. And *control is what attachment is all about!* These frequencies are very interconnected. They usually go hand in hand and feed off of each other, so you really can't deal with one without facing the others. For example, you can't feel separate without feeling some kind of fear or un-love-ability. You usually can't feel fear without there being some underlying limiting belief, like scarcity. And if you believe in scarcity, then that means you are holding a consciousness of separation. You are feeling separate from your Source – Infinite Oneness.

So how do you manage attachment? You manage the three amigos! When your ego is at the forefront of your attachment, the idea that you are separate from Source will promote the thought: "I am alone and have to take care of myself, because if I don't, nobody will." This illusion of separation will fuel your fear, and your fear will make you want to control things. You may find yourself wanting to control every detail of how your dream manifests. You may find yourself believing that the object of your attachment is the *only* answer to your dream or to your problem. **When your ego is fueling your attachment, replacement therapy is the tool that will allow you to remember that you are One with Source; that you are loved, safe and cared for always; and that if you allow it, your highest good will come to you – possibly in the form you imagined, or maybe differently and even better.**

When your emotions are fueling attachment, your consciousness of separation will likely activate all sorts of fear-based emotions, including anxiety, desperation, anger, hopelessness, etc. These fear-based emotions will activate your survival instinct to control. **The way to release the attachment when**

your emotions are getting the better of you is to harness their power through honoring them, allowing them to release, and consequently creating the space to allow Source to do its thing: to inspire you, guide you, heal you and bring you peace.

When your limiting beliefs are fueling your attachment, then thoughts of scarcity, limitation and conditionality are causing you to hold on tight to your imagined, limited third-dimensional reality. Belief in scarcity, limitation and conditionality leaves no room for an infinitely loving, powerful, and wise consciousness to express in your life. **When limiting beliefs are getting in the way, your best course of action is to identify them, challenge them, dismantle them and replace them with positive truths.**

What, Then, Do I Focus On!?

When you let go of attachment, you are letting go of control. You are letting go of your pictures – how you think your dream should look, or how it should happen. So, you may find yourself saying, "Well, then, what DO I focus on? You've had me fire up my Wanting Mechanism. You've had me identify what I want. You've got me believing I can have my dream. You've got me pretending. What do I focus on?" The answer...

> "Focus on the essence and the form will come."
> — *Leslie Kiernan*
> *spiritual teacher*

With practice, this mantra will keep you right on track with your dream, while helping you to fend off attachment.

Essence is defined as:
- The basic, real or invariable nature of a thing; substance.
- The true nature or constitution of anything.
- Something that exists, especially a spiritual or immaterial entity.

In other words, when you focus on the essence, you are focusing on the *vibration*. And if you are focusing on the vibration, you are focusing on the *feelings and qualities that your dream fulfilled would evoke.* For this reason, the Vision Workshop is extremely powerful, because it not only helps you identify what you want, but also, in writing and reading your vision, you are focusing on the *essence* of your dream. This is because a vision captures a state of *being*, not a way of *having*. You can *have* anything you want, but is that a guarantee it will make you happy? No.

Essence vs. Form

The following examples illustrate the powerful and important difference between focusing on the essence instead of being attached to the form.

Fancy Toys and Success

You may think that if you have a fancy SUV, $500 burning a hole in your pocket at any given time, and lots of impressive toys, *then* you'd be successful. So, you become really attached to having these things. You even find ways of buying them and you often experience waves of enjoying them. However, upon looking more deeply, you discover that an annoying, unidentifiable gnawing in your stomach is plaguing you. After you're done driving your cool car around, or impressing a lady with your generous spending, you face moments of quiet. With no fancy toys to distract you from how you are feeling, another reality creeps into your mind and gut. You are up to your eyeballs in debt. Your relationships with women leave a bad taste in your mouth. Your job pays your bills, but you hate it. You realize that your sense of success is totally dependent on whether or not you have a lot of cash at the moment or not. And ... "Darn it! What is it with my stomach? Am I getting an ulcer?" As you knead your fist into your stomach for the thousandth time, a little voice quietly whispers, "This is not a successful life." Your soul is talking.

This scenario is an example of being attached to pictures, and focusing on form vs. essence. When you decide to listen to your soul's guidance, rather than brush it off as you have a million times before, you realize you need to be willing to let go of your attachment to these fancy toys and look more deeply. Instead of making third-dimensional stuff the source of your success, you have the opportunity to identify and focus on the feelings and qualities you wish to experience and manifest in your life. When you make this shift a whole new world of possibility begins to reveal itself. You'll open the door to the Universe's guidance and begin experiencing all sorts of synchronistic happenings that lead you forward: you'll catch an inspirational talk-show guest on the radio, experience chance meetings with strangers who turn you on to the perfect book, you'll discover teachers, mentors, opportunities and classes that can help you discover what true success could feel and look like for you. When you let go of attachment, you accept the truth that success is an inside job and that it begins with a consciousness of success within.

Financially Secure Relationship

You may think you want financial security in the relationship of your dreams, and so you become attached to finding a man who makes a lot of money. You become attached to the picture of what financial security in a relationship looks like. And so, there could be hundreds of Mr. Rights in your vicinity, but you can't see them. Meanwhile, you go through numerous failed relationships with wealthy men, because you're trying to control how it happens. Or you manifest a relationship with a rich man, but you are not fulfilled. You got the financial security you thought you wanted, but because you were controlling how and what you would allow the Universe to give you, financial security is all you got. When, instead, you let go of attachment and let the Universe fulfill your dream for your highest and greatest good, you may discover what you really wanted in the name of financial security was a man you felt safe with, who would take care of you. Maybe instead of gaining financial security by marrying a man of means, you got a man you trusted with your life. The financial security came later and more meaningfully from the deep and powerful partnership you built with him. When you let go of attachment you are essentially saying to the Universe, "This or something better."

How John's Story Ends

Remember John and his gripping attachment to the loan? Well, I have a secret to share. John was my husband, Chris, and his wife was me, in the pursuit of our dream to own a vineyard and make wine. Yes, all that did happen to us. And over the course of five of the longest months of our lives, we battled with our desperate attachment. Trying to control everything. Trying to *make* things go our way. Trying to save ourselves, my mother, and our partner from what was feeling like the biggest potential mistake of our lives. Feeling responsible for uprooting my mother. Feeling weighted by having a portion of my sister's highly anticipated future inheritance tied up in this nightmare of a financial limbo. Spending our life savings and our partner's life savings in order to keep the businesses alive so that we could pay the rent we were being charged, with the chance we could lose it all if a loan didn't come through.

Many times, Chris and I found ourselves staring at each other in disbelief. We'd say, "How could this be happening? We're smart, capable people. We did our homework. How can we feel like victims when we don't hold a victim consciousness?" Yet, despite feeling powerless many times, we continued cycling through the unfolding pattern of talking with a loan broker, becoming hopeful, waiting, then getting turned down. Eventually, with each disheartening denial, we let go a little bit more, managing the three amigos as best we could, until finally we faced the reality that this could actually fall apart and there was nothing we could do about it. We slowly came to the conclusion that God may have another plan for us and we *let go*. Once we did, it became easier to listen for guidance, take *inspired* action (vs. ego-driven action), and put one foot in front of the other. We finally found ourselves saying, "Okay, God, you lead the way, cuz we obviously can't make this happen on our own." And, after five months of doing all we could do, we released it all and went to a family reunion in Texas. Five days into our trip, Chris got a call on his cell phone from the latest banker we were dealing with. The loan had been approved.

There is No Loss without a Greater Gain

> "When one door of happiness closes, another opens;
> but often we look so long at the closed door
> that we do not see the one which has been opened for us."
> — *Helen Keller (1880-1968)*
> *deaf-blind, American author, activist, lecturer*

Now, it is entirely possible that **no** loan was to come through and that the vineyard was **not** to be ours. We could just as easily have been put on another path. But I can guarantee you, *ultimately* the end result would have been even better than if our original dream had manifested. Why? Because, as Rev. David Alexander of New Thought Ministries of Oregon teaches us, "There is no loss without a greater gain." This is because, in line with its infinite nature, the Universe is always expanding. Yet, at the same time, like life expressing in human form, the Universe *breathes*. It expands and contracts, and expands and contracts. The contractions can be the hard times. The expansions can feel easier.

When you experience contraction in your life, it feels as if your life is contracting around you. You may feel that you have no power. That you are losing everything. Out of control in every way. In contrast, the experience of expansion brings feelings of power and control, as if you're in "the groove" and things are going your way. When you're going through a contraction, as we did during our five-month limbo, the important thing to remember is, "This too shall pass." And, if you stay out of your own way, if you stay open to Source as best you can by managing your human tendencies, instincts and states of consciousness, you'll experience expansion once again.

The trick to riding out the contraction periods is to suspend judging the contraction as bad. Remember, God is good all the time, and God is present even in your darkest hours. But if you start attaching *meaning* to the "bad" things that are happening, then you are using your divine creative power to make these things so! If you say, "What's happening is bad and it means I don't get to have my dreams," then, by the Law of Attraction, you'll get what you ask for – *you not getting* *your dreams.* You will have slammed the door in the Universe's face by judging the events. And once you begin to judge the events as bad, you are essentially becoming attached to them being bad!

Ultimate Loss

I feel that I cannot make the declaration: "There is no loss without a greater gain," without addressing the human perception of ultimate loss – death. Your response to my declaration might sound something like, "You're trying to tell me that the loss of my loved one will result in a greater gain? How sick is that?" And the answer is, "No, from the human, ego perspective, it is not possible to experience a greater gain from the loss of a loved one. However, the spiritual truths being articulated here are just that, *spiritual* truths. Which means that from the soul perspective, there indeed is a greater gain that can come from death."

There are endless resources for those who need or want to explore positive spiritual perspectives on death: the soul's opportunity to merge once again with the infinite nature of Source; the surviving loved one's opportunity for spiritual growth and development; the fulfillment of agreements made between loved ones before incarnating in this life, to name a few. But to address these deep philosophical questions within the context of this book would require another book. And, because we are here to discover how to step out of our own way in order to manifest our dreams, it benefits us more to explore how to manage our ego's relationship to loss.

Death and Rebirth

"All changes, even the most longed for, have their melancholy; for
what we leave behind is a part of ourselves; we must die to one
life before we can enter into another!"
— *Gail Sheehy (1937-)*
American author

A vital aspect to stepping out of your own way is to educate yourself and strive to accept the nature of the human experience. The human experience includes an infinite range of possibility – everything from complete bliss to devastating suffering. The human experience is the light and the dark, and to the degree you can accept the dark as a part of life, you are able to allow into your experience the light. Not only is physical death a part of life, but the experience of living is a continual process of little deaths followed by little births. Every time you learn something new and integrate it into your way of being, the *you* that you were before dies, and gives birth to a new *you* with greater wisdom. It is very common in the process of making big dreams come true, to have to let go of an aspect of yourself or your life that no longer fits in with the you who you must become for your dream to be realized.

- In order to be financially free, you must let die the part of yourself that doesn't want to be responsible, the part of you that believes in scarcity, that part of you that only knew poverty.
- In order to become a wife, you must let die that single woman who had only herself to think of.
- In order to become physically healthy and fit, you must let die that part of you that doesn't love yourself enough to commit to your well-being.
- In order to heal your body, you must let die the idea that you have no power to heal.
- In order to be a good mother, fully present with the miracle that is your child, you must let die that part of you that likes everything to be neat, tidy and perfect.

The process and the opportunity are the same, whether facing the ultimate loss of death or little deaths along the way to transformation. The only difference is the degree of difficulty. The only way to experience the greater gain that is available after a loss is to honor the loss itself. If the loss is not acknowledged, it cannot be released. And if it is not released, you become attached to the loss through your resistance of it. If your energy is focused on resisting the loss, your consciousness becomes stuck in the loss, unable to open up and receive the new possibility of the greater gain. So, when we get stuck in the trap of attachment, the path to freedom is through an empowering relationship with our emotions. We must feel. We must honor. We must release.

Getting Help

It is likely that stepping out of your own way is the hardest part of The Formula because you are dealing with yourself ... and you can't escape yourself. Ever hear the saying, "Wherever you go, there you are"? Well, this is the case with stepping out of your own way. Oftentimes, you may step out of your own way, only to meet the same you who you were stepping away from. So, it is highly recommended that you get help along the way. Outside help can offer you fresh eyes, a different perspective, new information, encouragement and support – the kind of energy you cannot access on your own.

The help available comes in many forms: therapy, healers, teachers, friends, classes, groups, books, tapes, etc. And within each form are different approaches – physical, spiritual, mental, psychic, psychological, holistic, allopathic, natural, technical, the list goes on. It would be overwhelming to find help if you thought there was a *right way*, but fortunately there is only *your way*.

When that little voice of inspiration tells you it's time to get help, let your soul guide you. Set your intention to find the right teacher, healer, guide or resource. Listen for guidance and then act on it. Above all else, trust your gut and follow your heart. Whatever *feels* right *is* right. And know that what is right for you today may not be right for you tomorrow. You may find a path that works for a while, but later you outgrow it. You may go through periods of solitude and periods of connecting with others. All of this adds up to the expansion process that allows you to integrate your ego, honor your emotions, transform limiting beliefs and let go of attachment, such that letting the Universe give you what you want becomes more effortless and natural as you evolve.

19

The Mystic's Journey

By now, you have probably gathered that Step III of The Mystic's Formula is more than just a step in making your dreams come true. It is a step that, when you truly surrender to the opportunity it presents, will change you. Beyond learning how to step out of your own way, Step III offers you a way of being.

As you travel the mystic's journey, you will visit four different stations. If this journey is new to you, each station may feel like strange and unfamiliar territory. However, if you stay on the path, you will find some familiarity and predictability along the way. On the mystic's journey, we travel the path with conscious intent. The four stations are not necessarily visited in any particular order and they often overlap. If your soul tells you there is value on this path – if you realize what you've been doing isn't working and your desire for a more expanded way is strong enough to stay the course – then you will visit the four stations over and again, evermore expanding your sense of self.

The Four Stations of the Mystic's Journey

- **Awakening** – When you enter the station of Awakening, you discover there are new and different possibilities available to you.
- **Study** – When you enter the station of Study, you find your teachers, you question and deconstruct your beliefs, you challenge old perspectives and outgrow your teachers, and you construct new beliefs based on your discoveries.

- **Integration** – When you enter the station of Integration, you begin to stand on your own two feet, independent of your past teachers and authority figures. You practice what you've come to know and believe, and discover what it means to be you (the reconstructed you) in the world.
- **Expression** – When you enter the station of Expression, you offer yourself to others, being your authentic self, fully-expressed.

Qualities of the Mystic

Step III of The Formula builds character. As you move through Step III, you will discover it's impossible to successfully manage your human tendencies, instincts, and states of consciousness without developing and drawing upon some qualities that demand your very best. These qualities will serve you well as you practice Step III. When you feel stuck, these qualities can guide you toward your next steps:

Openness – When you draw upon the quality of Openness, you let down your defenses. You are unprotected, accessible and responsive. You can allow in new possibilities.

Willingness – When you draw upon Willingness, you access your power to choose and are ready to act or allow.

Faith – When you draw upon Faith, you take risks. To travel the mystic's journey, you must often give up, at least temporarily, the things that give you security. Faith is belief that is not based on proof. When you practice faith, you are letting go of the things you've always trusted or held on to, and find a different aspect of yourself or life to trust in order to take the risk.

Commitment – When you draw upon Commitment, you take action. When you are committed, you give yourself in trust. You identify your intention and give yourself to a course of action you will follow through to completion, *no matter what*. You understand and trust that even if things do not go as you expected, *everything* that transpires is part of the journey.

Discipline – When you draw upon Discipline, you summon commitment, faith and a long-term perspective. When you are disciplined, you give yourself to an activity, exercise or regimen that develops or improves a skill. Usually the rewards you seek to experience through the discipline are not to be had until time has passed – often several to many years. Without discipline, the tools and techniques will remain *good ideas*, but true transformation will not be possible.

Courage – When you draw upon Courage, you are not fearless. To the contrary, to be courageous is, as author Susan Jeffers teaches, to "feel the fear and do it anyway." The more you develop a productive relationship with your fear, the easier it becomes to be courageous.

Honesty – When you draw upon Honesty you are truthful. Above all else, you must be honest with yourself, willing to face the truth about yourself, as only you can define it.

Purpose – When you draw upon Purpose, you access your reason for doing something. To be purposeful is to seek meaning and keep that meaning close to your heart at all times.

These are the qualities of the mystic. Use this list when you find yourself struggling with the *self-management* piece of *Stepping Out of Your Own Way*. If you're lost, look at this list and ask yourself, "How do I need to be right now?" If you sit quietly and listen, your soul will guide you. And more and more, you'll find you know just what to do.

THE MYSTIC'S FORMULA
Step IV:

Welcome It into Your Life

20

When Your Dream Arrives

Step IV of The Mystic's Formula, *Welcoming It into Your Life*, is about much more than welcoming your dream or your manifestation into your life. It is about welcoming into your life a new way of living, a new way of seeing life and the Universe. Remember, if this book were about mere achievement, Step IV would be: *Claim Your Bragging Rights and Go Out and Celebrate!* But because we're talking about a *transformational* approach to personal success, Step IV is about acknowledging, allowing and cultivating personal transformation, courtesy of the desire your dreams awaken within you.

If you follow Steps I, II and III of The Mystic's Formula, your dreams will indeed come true. They may look different than you originally envisioned. You may have been transformed by the journey, causing you to redefine your dream. Or you may have allowed the Universe to give you more or better than you could have ever imagined. Regardless of the form your dream takes, the essence of your dreams *must and will* manifest because of the unchangeable laws of the Universe:

- The Law of Attraction is always at work whether you like it or not.
- The nature if Spirit is ALL goodness.
- Source is ever-expanding.

By definition, this means, if you stay open and allow Source energy to express in, as, and through you, *you will always be guided toward your greatest good.*

When your dreams arrive, make sure you notice! Take pause. And give grateful thanks. It is amazing how often our dreams manifest and, after spending so much time and energy focusing on its manifestation, we briefly acknowledge it and quickly move on to the next topic that captures our longing. One of the reasons for this phenomenon is that by the time your dream manifests, your vibration is such a perfect match for it that it feels like the most natural thing in the world – the next most logical step in your life. There's nothing wrong with this. It is our nature and our purpose to create, and we must experience desire for the creative process to launch. We did not choose life in the third dimension to *have* things. We came here to *create* and *experience*. And so it is. As soon as we *have*, we're on to the next thing we want to have. But it is not the *having* that's pulling at us. It's actually our soul's calling to expand by creating and experiencing itself anew.

Yet, if you want to build on the momentum of the manifestation you've just experienced, give big thanks! Milk the gratitude vibration for all it's worth. Remember, gratitude is one of the most powerful manifestation vibrations you can hold. And as you catch the gratitude wave, let its power build ever-increasing momentum and carry you toward your next desire. As you desire more, let yourself enjoy the desire, let yourself want what you want. Go back to Part I of The Mystic's Formula and let The Mystic's Formula work its magic again and again and again. *But also know this:* The Mystic's Formula offers so much more than a way to make your earthly dreams come true. It offers you the opportunity to expand your consciousness. And if you choose to go there, great and wondrous things await you.

21

Transformation Awaits You

Now, before I go on with all that awaits you, let me be perfectly clear about one thing: If all you do is follow The Mystic's Formula and make your dreams come true for the rest of your life, you will have lived life well. And that is something to be proud of! However, if you want to *Welcome into Your Life* ALL that is waiting for you, the sky's the limit.

What awaits you beyond the manifestation of your dreams is transformation. Transformation is not about *changing* who you are but *discovering* who you are, deep inside, beneath the layers of parental conditioning, societal expectations, the environment you grew up in and the traumas that wounded you along the way. Transformation happens when you begin the process of freeing yourself from the limitations that bind you, to discover your true nature as a divine being, a co-creator. When people use The Mystic's Formula to make their dreams come true, concepts that their analytical mind could only conceive of, become palpable experiences. People begin to:

- Discover a faith rooted in deep understanding, not blindly held by fragile wishful-ness.
- Feel a greater power lovingly expressing through their lives.
- Experience more ease and grace, releasing fight and struggle.
- Become more present in the now, rather than living in the past or the future.

- Really get that the conditions of their lives are just an illusion and the only thing that's real is consciousness.
- Understand that the life they desire comes more from *being* than *doing*.
- Experience and express more meaning in their lives.
- Deeply feel their connection to All That Is.

The Flip Phenomenon

One way you might experience transformation during Step IV of The Mystic's Formula is that your priorities may *flip*. You may discover that what was important to you before has evolved. For many people who follow a metaphysical approach to their dreams, there is an interesting *before and after* phenomenon that looks something like this:

Before

Your priority is the realization of your dream and developing a close and personal relationship with Spirit is a means to an end.

   Then FLIP...

After

A close and personal relationship with God has now become your priority and the expression of your dreams is a vehicle to become closer to God.

If this happens for you, it means you have expanded.

To Me, By Me, Through Me, As Me

Contemporary theological teachings known as New Thought address four stages of spiritual growth. The first stage is the **To Me** consciousness. This level of consciousness has you perceive life through an awareness of victimhood. The To Me perception has you believe that life happens *to you*. You may feel powerless to create the life you desire, or that you are at the mercy of circumstances or fate. Yet because the One consciousness is always expanding, and your consciousness is part of the One, the opportunity to expand beyond To Me is always there.

In order to move out of victimhood, you must discover the consciousness of dominion. Here, you begin to understand the Universal law of cause-and-effect. Your understanding is based in the concept that things happen **By Me**. Your desires are likely to be dictated by your ego as you exert your own authority over life conditions. Your openness to, or trust of, a greater power may be conditional and tenuous. You may see glimmers of what it can be like to really allow Source energy to do all the work, but you'd still rather be in control.

As you expand to the **Through Me** consciousness, you begin to experience Source working *through you*. Your awareness is one of partnership with Source. This usually occurs when something in you has let go or healed. Your faith deepens as you begin to know you are loved all the time – that you don't need to control everything because you are safe. You can trust that God wants you to have all that is good. Your ego becomes more integrated. And, as you let go of control, you have more and more evidence of good unfolding for you, even when life looks differently than you planned. You watch your life unfold with awe and enthusiasm. And when things don't go as expected, you think, "Hmmm, I wonder what the Universe is manifesting for me now."

The final stage is the **As Me** consciousness. This state is one of surrender and enlightenment. At this level, you relax into the Allness of life. You live from the consciousness that you are One with the Infinite.

The Flip Phenomenon is not as black and white as it sounds. It is actually more of a door opening. You may find yourself expanding into higher states of consciousness as you move through the To Me, By Me, Through Me, and As Me perceptions. However, once you become aware of what's possible you may move back and forth between the different states of consciousness, depending on what's going on in your life.

For example, you may have expanded from the victim mentality of To Me to the more empowered consciousness of By Me, willing to explore your responsibility in the happenings of your life. You may hang out in this state of self-responsibility, when *bam* something particularly challenging occurs. You may find yourself incapable of reactivating that sense of creative empowerment, and feeling victimized as you ask, "How could this happen to me?"

Or you may have expanded into a Through Me consciousness, living your life generally surrendered to and trusting that Source is always guiding you to your greatest good, making manifest wondrous things in your life, taking care of your every need, when *Bam*, something particularly challenging happens and you try to take control of the situation. You find yourself not so trusting that good is expressing even in this difficult time. Your ego gathers strength and you find yourself feeling separate, alone and do, do, doing all you can to change the circumstances of your life.

Fear is generally the culprit when you feel yourself contract into a less expansive way of perceiving your life, and the *three amigos* are usually in the mix. This, then, makes the contraction experience an opportunity to practice managing your human tendencies, instincts and states of consciousness. What usually happens is that each contraction is followed by a more expanded consciousness – a "two-steps-forward, one-step-back," or, "three-steps-forward, two-steps-back" phenomenon. As you continue expanding in this way, you find yourself contracting to the more narrow perception less often, and for a shorter duration. And it becomes easier and easier to remember what you already know – the higher state of consciousness. Now **that** is transformation!

Sense of Self

Another transformational possibility, in addition to the Flip Phenomenon, is that you may experience an evolution in your self-identity. For example, with Step IV of The Mystic's Formula, you may evolve from an identity based in **Who I Am** to **How I'm Being**. Both methods of self-definition are wonderful and satisfying. The difference is simply a matter of consciousness and an opportunity for expansion. One is not better or worse than the other.

The Who I Am identity is an expression of the By Me consciousness. The Who I Am person operates more in the third dimension, with less of a calling to explore their sensitivity to the nonphysical realm. Their sense of personal fulfillment may still come from a fair share of ego gratification. Their sense of self may be significantly connected with what they have achieved or accomplished. And the opinions of others may still be fairly important to the Who I Am identity.

If, however, you're called to expand into the How I'm Being way of defining yourself, it is usually because you are beginning to experience some dissatisfaction with the Who I Am identity. You may find yourself lonely or feeling disconnected from others at times. You may find that ego-gratification isn't enough to feel fulfilled. You may find that the approval of others isn't giving you what you'd hoped for. When you begin to feel dissatisfied, you'll start to let go of your attachment to these ways of defining yourself. And when you let go, there is a void. The void is good, for it creates a space for new possibilities, courtesy of Source energy's infinite supply. Since Source's nature is abundant, generous, loving, joyful, peaceful and easy, etc., these ways of being can now start to seep into your awareness. You may begin to see glimmers of a new way of defining yourself. You may want to experience these ways of being more and more, because these *feelings* are the things you were wanting all along when you were living in your Who I Am identity. And so, as you begin to see that, then your sense of self can come from allowing the One consciousness to express in, as, and through you.

When you make this shift, then *how you're being* becomes more important than *who you are*. If you are experiencing positive feelings, then you know that must mean you're allowing more of the One consciousness to flow through you. Remember the One consciousness is *all* good. So if you are moving more toward feeling all good, it means you are allowing more and more Source energy in. **This focus on *how you are feeling* increases your desire to consciously *choose how you are being*. This is because you cannot *be* joyful and *feel* sad. You cannot *be* generous and *feel* cheated. You cannot *be* peaceful and *feel* stressed.** And so, as you practice being more of how you want to be, *Who You Are* expands from what you look like to the outside world to who you are being in your internal world.

Expanding the Transformational Experience

Once you've begun to experience transformation, you can never again *not know* what you *now know*. You have expanded. You are bigger than you were before. And so what is now satisfying will no longer fit into the smaller life of before. A very common and challenging aspect of expansion is that you may feel lost – as if you're in a void – or uncomfortable because the old way of being is gone but the new way of being isn't quite here yet. Your personality may want to return to what is familiar. But what usually happens is that when you try, you are quickly reminded that the old way no longer fits. You will likely experience many different emotions as you expand – everything from emptiness, fear, and stagnation to joy, freedom, and enthusiasm. Whatever the emotions, you now have the tools to deal with them. Keep practicing harnessing the power of your emotions, and know that the best way to move toward the unknown is by listening and taking guidance from your Wanting Mechanism. Keep identifying what you want as you transform and expand, and your next steps will reveal themselves.

Whether you are eagerly looking for what to do next with your expansion, or you happen to feel like you're in the void, one of the most helpful things you can do is to *choose a path* for this chapter of your life. If, in your expansion process, you are feeling enthusiastic and crystal clear, choosing a path will be easy. Your Wanting Mechanism will be joyfully driving the bus and you'll find yourself freely attacking growth opportunities with zest. If, however, you feel overwhelmed, lost, or in the void, choosing a path is that much more important, for it will bring focus and direction to your expansion process.

Do not allow yourself to simply stay busy just because you don't know what to do. Sometimes, when you are in the void, what is called for is *simply being* in the void. You may feel unmotivated to take any next steps. Trust in the void. Although there may be no transformational fireworks to be seen, things do change at the unconscious level and you'll be guided as to when the time is right for more movement. The void is a powerful time to listen for guidance and really let your soul guide you in taking your next steps. What follows are some of the paths you may want to explore as you create direction or purpose for your continued expansion.

The Path of Self-Healing

When you embrace a transformational approach to personal success, you often discover you might have some healing work to do. As you practice letting yourself want what you want, pretending you already have it, and mindfully managing your human tendencies, instincts and states of consciousness, you will often find there are blocks, wounds and areas of stuck-ness you keep hitting. You may find yourself either unable to move beyond a certain point, or returning to the same old wound over and over again. The bad news is, these barriers are no fun. The good news is, the pursuit of your dreams has brought you to the opportunity to once and for all heal these areas. And there is so much out there to help you do just that. Here are a few helpful hints if you decide your next step in your transformational journey is to do some healing work:

Get Help

Albert Einstein said, "The world we have made, as a result of the level of thinking we have done thus far, creates problems we cannot solve at the same level of thinking at which we created them." This means, if you approach your healing without input from a new source outside yourself, all you have in your healing efforts is *your* consciousness. And *your* consciousness is the same one that perpetuates any problems you may have. If you are going to shake up your old perspective and acquire new information and skills to find a new way of relating to an old wound, then you must get help. If you are called to do some healing work, do yourself a favor and dedicate yourself to finding the right fit. There are many kinds of help out there, just as there are many levels of expertise and professional integrity. What follows are some guidelines to help you find the help you may be seeking.

Explore Unusual Resources

Books are great resources and many of us rely on them for learning but they are limited in that they generally leave you intellectualizing and analyzing things from a cerebral perspective. Intellectual wisdom is great for intellectual problems, but you need emotional wisdom to heal emotional problems, spiritual wisdom to heal spiritual problems ... you get the idea. If you really want to heal, you must be willing to be uncomfortable and try things that may seem weird or unorthodox to you. Although it is impossible to list all the wonderful modalities for healing out there, here are some just to heighten your awareness:

- Counseling
- Energy Healing and Energy Psychology
- Hypnosis
- Neuro-Linguistic Programming (NLP)
- Acupuncture
- Bodywork
- Art Therapy
- Movement Therapy

Trust Your Heart, Check Your Gut

You may ask, "How do I begin to find a healing venue, and when I do, how do I know if it's the right one?" There's a saying: "When the student is ready the teacher appears," and nothing could be more true. This phenomenon is a perfect example of letting yourself want what you want and allowing the Universe to give it to you. Just tell the Universe, "Okay, Source, send me what I need." When you are ready for healing, the right circumstances, resources, conversations and people will show up. And once they begin to show up, it is important to know there is no *right* healing venue. There is only the right one for you.

The only way to know if a particular modality or practitioner is right for you is to trust your gut. It is possible for a practitioner to look great on paper, have all the right diplomas and credentials, and still *not* be right for you. Check your gut. Conversely, it is possible for your mind to be skeptical, building a case against a particular person or method, but when you check your gut, something may be nudging you to continue. Remember, your mind is the ego's powerful tool used to preserve the status quo. Your ego wants to maintain power in your life, but when you bring your attention to your heart and your gut, you *feel* things. And since emotions are the language of the soul, you'll know your soul is guiding you when you *feel in your gut* that the practitioner or method is right for you.

The Tribal Path

Another phenomenon that often occurs when you begin to expand is that you may find the people you used to hang out with might not be able to support you in your transformation. You may feel you are outgrowing your friends. You may start to feel disconnected from them, or that you seem to have less and less in common. You may feel lonely even when you are surrounded by those who are familiar. You may feel your friends and/or family don't *get who you are*. All of these experiences can be challenging and you may feel lonely. But hopefully your consciousness will have expanded enough to know that these feelings have nothing to do with your lovability or worth. Rather, these are growing pains.

Again, it is invaluable to practice the tools for harnessing the power of your emotions. Honor your feelings. Find productive and responsible avenues of expression and release. Then listen. Listen for guidance. Know there *are* people out there who are like-minded and like-hearted. There are souls out there who will *get you*. And, if your next step in your journey is to find those souls, then so be it. Find your tribe! Go back to Step I. Identify what kinds of relationships you want. Own it. And swiftly move on to Step II. Start pretending you have it. Watch how fast you start attracting the right people in your life. Listen for guidance. Take inspired action. Sometimes it takes patience, but you just never know when a kindred spirit may come into your life! It happens all the time. Below are a few easy ways to get the tribal drums beating in your life:

Take a class aligned with your current area of expansion. If, for example, your expansion has led you to discover that your soul's purpose is to create empowering growth experiences for teenagers, take a class that will help you learn more about how to do that. Don't take just any class that has nothing to do with where you're going in your life just to meet people.

Join a club. Same rules apply here as with taking a class. Remember, you have a purpose. You have a direction for this time of expansion. Keep listening to your soul's guidance.

Start your own special interest group. If you build it, they will come. If you can't find what you're looking for, create it. All it takes to form a group of like-minded people is: a) one person to own it, and b) another person to join in. Poof! Two people makes a group. Then pretend you already have it. Start meeting regularly, doing what you want to do. Keep sharing what you're doing with others and invite them as it feels right. This is, after all, how every group that ever existed ever came to be.

The Path of the Student

The next step in your transformational journey may be one of learning. As you expand, you may feel as if you've only just begun to scratch the surface regarding subjects you find compelling. Or you may be in the void feeling there is just so much more to know. Whatever the motivation, the path of the student is a very useful and productive one to claim. And, much like the path of self-healing, there is no right teacher or class – just the right one for you. Here again the key is to identify what you want to learn by listening to your Wanting Mechanism, and letting the clarity of your desire guide you to allow the right teachers, classes or experiences into your life. Trust your gut and listen to your heart as you study. You may find yourself dabbling in a variety of different studies, gathering more and more learning without knowing what to do with it for quite some time. Or you may zero in on and immerse yourself in an area of study that takes hold of your passion for an extended period of time. The key is always to follow what *feels* right. Keep listening to and trusting your soul's guidance. Remember, when you feel good, that is your soul telling you you're right on track. And

when you feel bad, that is your soul telling you that you're thinking thoughts contrary to your deeper knowing.

The Path of Service

"However many holy words you read, however many you speak,
what good will they do you if you do not act upon them?"

— *Buddha*

The path of service is a powerful, beautiful and meaningful one
for expansion. Service is all about giving. It is powerful because
giving, like gratitude, expresses the high vibration of: "I HAVE
and I AM." When you give, you express the vibration of: "I have
love to give, I have time to give, I have talents to give, I am
loving, I am generous, I am valuable."

Many transformational experiences can unfold through being of service, *if* you have the correct intention behind the service. In order for service to contribute to your expansion, you
must enter into service willing to give generously. You must
give without expectation of anything in return, give for the sake
of giving, give without thought of yourself, give without strings
attached, and give without keeping score regarding what you're
getting back. The quality of giving is not in the amount you give,
but in *how you are being* when you give. As Mother Teresa taught
us, "It is not the magnitude of our actions but the amount of
love that is put into them that matters."

Because giving expresses the *I have* and *I am* vibration, it is
guaranteed that you will receive much through giving. The Law
of Attraction makes it so. The irony is, it sounds contradictory
to say in the same breath, "Through giving you will receive,"
and, "You must give without any thought of yourself." The key
is this: It is one thing to have your desires *motivate* you to give,
and an entirely different thing to give as a way of *getting*. If self-
interest motivates you to be of service, great! "Yahoo!" for self-
interest. Self-interest and ego are great motivators, after all.
But once you're motivated to give, then let yourself learn how to
really give! Know it is in fully surrendering yourself to the experience of service that you will be transformed.

The possibilities for growth through service are many. If you've never before given selflessly, you will awaken and discover a part of yourself that you have never before experienced. Giving freely opens the heart so you may experience love in ways you've never known. If you've never given selflessly before, or have only known survival, self-interest or obligation, it is likely your ego or your wounds have played a big role in your life. When you start to give, and stretch to be of true service, your ego and your wounds will be revealed to you. Giving helps you integrate your ego. Giving helps you heal yourself. Your ego would have you believe that, in giving, you will lose the thing that you give. However, through service, you discover you are filled and blessed by that which you give. Being of service will reveal limiting thoughts and judgments – about yourself, about others, about life and about the nature of the Universe. Once you uncover limiting beliefs, you then have the opportunity to challenge them and determine the deeper truth available for discovery.

Being of service will also activate the manifestation vibration. Again, the seeming contradiction appears: "If I'm to be other-focused, of selfless service, why should I care about manifesting things in my own life?" The truth is, once you *really get it* about service, manifesting things will no longer become the motivating factor it was. Instead, you will manifest your desires as a natural by-product of living a life of giving – where your consciousness consistently expresses the vibration of *I have*. Things you want and need will simply come to you, with little effort.

And so it is with the path of service. If you give freely, you will expand. You will discover and tap into all the unseen abundance that lives within you. You will circulate it freely, and it will come back to you multiplied.

Prayer of St. Francis

> *Lord, make me an instrument of your peace.*
> *Where there is Hatred, let me sow Love.*
> *Where there is Injury, Pardon.*
> *Where there is Doubt, Faith.*

Where there is Despair, Hope.
Where there is Darkness, Light, and
Where there is Sadness, Joy.

O Divine Master,
Grant that I may not so much
seek to be consoled as to console;
To be understood, as to understand;
To be loved, as to love;
For it is in giving that we receive,
It is in pardoning that we are pardoned,
And it is in dying that we are born to Eternal Life.

As Saint Francis understood, the path to freedom, wholeness and abundance is the path of giving. If you seek money, give money. If you seek love, give love. If you seek connection, then offer connection. If you seek health, be healthy. If you seek harmony, bring harmony. Whatever it is that's missing in your life, you must give it, offer it, bring it. For it is *your* consciousness that creates your experience. You cannot experience love when your consciousness contemplates pettiness. You cannot experience peace when your consciousness harbors resentments. You cannot experience abundance when you focus on lack. You cannot experience health when you focus on the fatality statistics your doctor recites. You cannot experience a sense of belonging when you hold yourself apart by focusing on the differences between you and others.

How to Choose Where to Give

The path of service may be calling you, but you may not know where to give. The good news is, there is no wrong way to choose. If your soul is nudging you, listen. There may be a certain population or cause that really pulls at your heart strings. Trust that. **It is not where you give or what you give that matters. It is that you give and *how you* give that matters.** Volunteer with elderly, children, animals, at church or through special interest organizations, for example. Volunteer for environmental causes, educational programs, the poor, the hungry, the sick or the homeless.

There is no right place to give, only your way to give. And *everyone* has something to give. You may be a business man who works 80 hours a week and think you may have no time to show up at a homeless shelter. But, in speaking to the shelter director, you discover they need someone to help them with a budgeting project. Perfect for you! "I can do that at my office," you think. Or you're a full-time mother of three, so you can't volunteer at school because that would require childcare for your little ones. But you discover that the fundraising committee needs someone to make phone calls. "I can do that from home," you think.

And one more pearl of wisdom about giving: although it is immensely satisfying to see results through your giving, know that many times, you may not. If, when being of service, you find yourself discouraged by the lack of a positive outcome, there is great opportunity to revisit your reason for being of service. Sometimes the opportunity is to explore whether or not your ego is in the picture. Your ego may be attached to recognition. Your ego may worry about how the result, or lack of result, reflects on you. Your ego may just want to feel the glory of an achievement. All these possibilities provide opportunities for growth and expansion.

Other times, the project or goal may be bigger than something you can see realized in your lifetime. Or you are looking in the wrong place to see whether or not you're making a difference. The result you seek may not be the result the organization seeks to realize in the grand scheme of things, but when you look up close, rather than at the big picture or into the future, you realize you made small differences in the lives of many individuals, and possibly a big difference in the lives of a few. When you give, you activate the highest vibrations of Source, which ripples out in ways you may never know.

22

There Is Only Oneness

"We invent nothing, truly. We borrow and recreate. We uncover and discover. All has been given, as the mystics say. We have only to open our eyes and hearts, to become one with that which is."

— Henry Miller (1891-1980)
American writer and painter

I remember many years ago hearing words that went something like this:

There is only Oneness.

My brain heard the words, but that's as far as it got. This idea seemed important to me on some level but I had no idea what it meant. The concept kept weaving its way in and out of my consciousness as I lived my life. Along the journey, I'd hear nice little sayings that seemed to be related to this supposedly profound concept, but they all sounded like platitudes:

- We are all connected.
- When you hurt another you are hurting yourself.
- It is in the giving that you receive.
- What goes around comes around.

But the deeper understanding of interconnected Oneness just kept eluding me. I couldn't wrap my brain around it. Then one day, I heard of an ocean metaphor and my soul really took hold of the awareness and expanded upon it ...

Imagine you are a drop in the ocean. As a drop, you have your own unique identity. Yet, you are made up of the same substance as all the rest of the ocean. There is no separation between you and the other drops. In your connection with other drops, you form the ocean. Although you are one with the ocean, you have the free will to do as you please, creating new experiences, changing form, moving in and out of different existences.

Sometimes you choose to dance in the vast Oneness of the ocean. Sometimes you choose to change form, evaporating into the atmosphere, exploring the world of air and clouds. You may choose yet another experience, becoming a raindrop that falls to Earth. Maybe you explore the snow experience. Maybe you join with several trillion of your friends to stretch beyond the ocean experience to become a river for a while. Maybe you become drinking water and explore the experience of being inside a plant, animal or human being. You may experience yourself as a hydrating fluid, as blood, as sweat, as urine. Maybe you join the liquids of the sewage system. And maybe you go back to the ocean. Whatever choices you make, whatever experiences you have, a few things remain constant.

1. You are never separate from the ocean. You may feel disconnected. You may forget you are part of the ocean. But you are still one with the ocean. You are still made up of the same substance as the ocean. The essence of what you are will never change, but the experiences you have, based on the choices you make, allow you to experience yourself anew forever more.

2. Because you are a part of the whole, what you do as an individual drop affects the experience of the entire ocean. If you evaporate, the ocean is changed. If you migrate through a purification system, the ocean is changed once again. If you move inland, part of the ocean becomes a river. No experience is good or bad, simply different. And with each individual choice or experience, the ocean evolves in its understanding and experience of itself. The form of the ocean changes, but the essence of it remains constant. And because you and all the other drops of

water are connected as part of the ocean, you influence each other and affect the ocean with every choice you make. For you are all a part of the ocean. You are one with the ocean.

And so it is with you and your relationship to Life – your relationship to Source – your relationship to All That Is. That drop of water is you, and the ocean is All That Is. Not only does your consciousness create your reality, but it influences the reality of the collective. This is great news because it means you are that powerful and a victim to no one and no thing. It also means that when you pursue your dreams – the things that fulfill you – not only will you be happier for it, but you also contribute to the whole and everyone benefits! For what we feel is contagious and influences those around us.

When you begin to grasp the concept that there is only One and you are a part of the whole – that there is no separation;

And when you begin to grasp the concept that the essential nature of this One is All-Good, All-Powerful, All-Knowing, All-Loving, Complete, and Infinite – that there is absolutely *nothing lacking* that could ever be needed or desired;

And when you begin to grasp the concept that there is no separation between you and this One ...

Then you can begin to grasp that anything and everything you could ever desire already exists, and that the only thing you need to do to experience it is to *allow* yourself to remember your Oneness with it.

THAT is the transformational power of wanting your dreams, pursuing your dreams, and manifesting your dreams. For it is in pursuing the thing you think will make you happy (i.e., your dream) that you are forced to remember that the Source of your happiness is Source itself, not the external dream. And it is in seeking to remember the true source of your happiness that you rejoin with Source. When you do that, *it is done.* There is no longer any separation between you and all you desire, for you have come home to yourself, and all that you desire has been right there waiting for you all along.

Epilogue

Remember when, at the beginning of this book, I spoke to you of how easy it is to read a book, have a few intellectual "Aha" moments, and have nothing to show for your new level of understanding? Well, upon completing this book, you are now at a defining moment. Will you do anything with what you've learned, or simply close the book and move on to your next cerebral playground?

I'm not criticizing *thinking* itself. God knows, I've been known among my friends to be the "headly girl." **But thinking without commitment, thinking without action, thinking without risk, *will change nothing in your life.*** You might be at a loss as to how exactly to take your next step. Maybe you've never really been the action-oriented type. Maybe you feel overwhelmed by your life, or because there is so much in this book, you don't know where or how to start. Maybe your limiting beliefs about creating change in your life are getting the better of you. Whatever the case, I have some suggestions that will help you to make the most of this defining moment.

If you want to take full advantage of the golden opportunity you have before you …

1. Go back to the table of contents or skim through the book and pick ONE thing that you feel good about.
2. Then DO that thing for as long as it feels good.
3. Then pick another thing that you feel good about.
4. And DO that thing for as long as it feels good, etc.

As long as you let yourself be guided by what feels good, by the Law of Attraction, you will continue to attract to you things you feel good about. Of course, there will be times on your journey that won't feel so good, but: a) you now have the tools to deal with this predictable aspect of manifesting success for the soul, and b) there is a difference between feeling bad because you are growing (this is productive pain) and feeling bad because you are resisting (this is unproductive pain).

There are countless, wonderful resources for you to explore as you contemplate what's next for you. If you want to learn more about how to use The Mystic's Formula to manifest specific dreams, you can find an ever-expanding list of resources and products at: **www.successforthesoul.com**.

Also, the Recommended Resources section that follows is a great place to consider possible next steps. This list doubles as an annotated bibliography. You'll easily get a sense of what each resource is about. You'll find books, movies, websites and organizations.

As, Abraham-Hicks says,
> **"You can never get it done,**
> **and you can never get it wrong."**

And remember:
> **"Do what you can."**

So, don't focus on getting it done. Just focus on what feels good and let that guide you toward joyful, inspired action!

ENJOY!

Bibliography/
Recommended Resources

The following list is by no means comprehensive, but it is a short and selective list of some of my favorite resources. Enjoy!

Books & Audio

Abraham-Hicks

A nonphysical collective of teachers known as Abraham are channeled by Esther Hicks. Providing a wealth of information about our energetic universe and how we co-create our experience, good places to start include the website - *www.abraham-hicks.com* or the following three books:
- *The Law of Attraction*
- *Ask and It Is Given*
- *The Amazing Power of Deliberate Intent*

Barbara DeAngelis, Ph.D.

- *Are You the One for Me? Knowing Who's Right and Avoiding Who's Wrong* – This book can help you become more effective in choosing the right mate by understanding successful and unsuccessful patterns in relationships.

Carole Dore

Dore dismantles some of the misconceptions around metaphysics that have people visualizing and affirming themselves into frustration. Her understanding and teaching of visualization is deep and effective.
- *Visualization – The Power of Your Heart!* – This audio package provides fun and powerful explanations of how to do visualization so that it really works.

- *The Emergency Handbook for Getting Money Fast* – A great resource, filled with tools and techniques to get the money flowing in your life.
- *The Intensified Prosperity Workshop* – When you're ready to identify and dissolve your money barriers and go to the next level in your prosperity consciousness, this audio package is priceless!
- *The PowerVision Contemplation Audios* – Play these as often as you can to shift your creative energy from what you don't want in your life toward what you do want. Really helps to shift your consciousness.

Wayne Dyer, Ph.D.

- *The Power of Intention: Learning to Co-Create Your World Your Way* – Easy to understand delivery teaches how to set the Universe in motion through the conscious use of your intention.

Dr. Masaru Emoto

- *The Hidden Messages in Water* – Amazing scientific research demonstrating how thoughts affect our physical reality.

Neville Goddard

Neville's metaphysical teachings are still refreshing, even 50 years after his career peaked. Check out these books for a consciousness-altering perspective on manifestation and God.

- *Your Faith is Your Fortune* – A metaphysical interpretation of the Bible.
- *Awakened Imagination* – Understand how your imagination is the gateway of reality.
- *Law and the Promise* – Filled with actual case studies of ordinary people manifesting extraordinary things through the power of visualization.
- *Power of Awareness* – Understand more deeply how you have the power to create your own reality.

Herb Goldberg, Ph.D.

- *What Men Really Want* – In order for women to have successful relationships with men, they need to understand, accept and respect the differences between men and women. This book provides the in-depth insight to make that possible.

Louise Hay

Long-standing bestselling author, Louise Hay offers powerful resources for understanding how our thoughts and emotions can directly affect our physical health. Her materials are a rich resource of tools and techniques to activate your power to heal yourself.

- *You Can Heal Your Life* – A great first book for understanding the undeniable body-mind connection.
- *Love Yourself, Heal Your Life Workbook* – A great way to begin practicing and implementing the tools explained in *You Can Heal Your Life.*

Harville Hendrix, Ph.D.

- *Getting the Love You Want – A Guide for Couples* – One of the most powerful resources for getting to the root of your relationship struggles. Complete with invaluable exercises, this book goes deep, yet is completely accessible.

Ellen Kreidman, Ph.D.

- *Single No More – How to Find Your Perfect Mate* – A great nuts and bolts resource for single women who want to create their dream relationship.

Robert Kiyosaki

Kiyosaki helps shift money paradigms that keep people stuck in the "rat-race." In concrete ways, his books address the changes necessary to expand your financial world for the better.

- *Rich Dad, Poor Dad: What the Rich Teach Their Kids About Money That the Poor and Middle Class Do Not!* – In fun parable form, this book addresses fundamental attitudes about money. If you're new to expanding your prosperity consciousness, it can provide a much needed wake-up call!

- *The Cash Flow Quadrant* – The quadrants address the money mind-sets of the Employee, the Self-Employed, the Investor and the Business Owner. To learn about the differences is to tap into that which can empower you financially.
- *Rich Dad's Guide to Investing: What the Rich Invest in that the Poor and Middle Class Do Not!* – Building on the previous two in greater depth. An opportunity to continue expanding your prosperity consciousness.

Bruce Lipton, Ph.D.

- *The Biology of Belief: Unleashing the Power of Consciousness, Matter and Miracles* – Cell biologist Dr. Lipton conveys scientific discoveries which demonstrate how the cells of the body are affected by our thoughts.

Dr. Phil McGraw

- *Relationship Rescue* – Whether you're in a relationship that needs help or seeking to create one that works, this book gives hands-on tools that can absolutely help you get there – IF you're willing to do the work!

Lynne McTaggart

- *The Field: The Quest for the Secret Force of the Universe* – A wonderful resource for those who want to understand Source Energy and consciousness in a more concrete way. Without getting overly scientific, McTaggart introduces the reader to the latest discoveries which point to a unifying energy structure, the *Zero Point Field*. As an investigative journalist she addresses a variety of interrelated subjects ranging from biology to astrophysics, medicine and the paranormal in an enlightening and accessible way.

Carolyn Myss

- *Anatomy of the Spirit* – A wonderful introduction for understanding the interaction between the different aspects of ourselves; the physical, mental, emotional and spiritual.

Michael Newton, Ph.D.

- *Journey of Souls: Case Studies of Life Between Lives* - Compiled from over 30 years of hypnotherapy regression cases, this work reveals uncannily consistent accounts of life in the spirit realm.

Carol Emery Normandi, Laurelee Roark

These authors guide you through the real issues underlying food and body issues – with hope, wisdom and compassion.
- *It's Not About Food: Change Your Mind; Change Your Life; End Your Obsession with Food and Weight* – An invaluable resource for those wanting a life beyond food, diets and scales.

James Oschman

- *Energy Medicine: The Scientific Basis* – Written by a well-known scientist with a background in biophysics and biology, this book brings together evidence to provide explanations for the energetic exchanges that take place in all therapies.

Candace Pert, Ph.D.

- *Molecules of Emotion: The Science Behind Mind-Body Medicine* – Research professor, Dr. Pert, establishes the biomolecular basis for our emotions. Discover how your psychology determines your physical well-being.

John Randolph Price

- *The Abundance Book* – Explains what the true source of all prosperity is and how to tap into it through consciousness. Includes the powerful 40-Day Prosperity Program.

- *Superbeings* – A Superbeing is a human being who has tapped into the unlimited power each of us holds. This book demonstrates how to become free from limitations and access infinite well-being.

Dave Ramsey

This author offers numerous no-nonsense resources for getting your financial life on track. As someone who has lost it all and did it right the second time around, Ramsey teaches you how to achieve financial fitness and pass this legacy on to your children.

- *The Total Money Makeover: A Proven Plan for Financial Fitness* – If you need a concrete plan and inspiration to move out of debt toward wealth management, this is the place to start.
- *Financial Peace Revisited* – A road map for financial security.
- *Financial Peace Jr. – Teaching Kids About Money* – Great hands-on tools to help your kids establish a lifetime of healthy financial habits. Good for kids 3–12.

Geneen Roth

- *Breaking Free from Emotional Eating* – If you're sick and tired of being sick and tired of diets and compulsive eating, this book offers tools that can set you free!
- *Why Weight? A Guide to Ending Compulsive Eating* – Filled with highly effective, transformational exercises, this is the next logical step to Breaking Free.

Michael Talbot

- *Holographic Universe* – For those who think energy healing and the paranormal are a bunch of New Age hooey, this book provides important research from credible scientists to support and explain the unexplainable. A great first exposure to quantum physics.

Neal Donald Walsch

Ever feel that religion and spirituality contradict each other? Walsch provides rich opportunities to continue finding your truth and experiencing validation for what you have felt in your heart.

- *Conversations with God: An Uncommon Dialogue (Book I)* – Addresses your personal relationship with the Infinite.
- *Conversations with God: An Uncommon Dialogue (Book II)* – Explores opportunities to express spiritual principles through government, economics, education...
- *Conversations with God: An Uncommon Dialogue (Book III)* – Explains how the Universe works.
- *Home With God: In a Life That Never Ends* – Asks and answers humanity's questions about life and death.

Organizations & Web Sites

- *Association for Comprehensive Energy Psychology (ACEP)* – This organization validates that energy work offers legitimate modalities for healing and transformation. Resources include a membership directory of licensed mental health professionals who practice and endorse energy psychology, books, classes, articles and more. *www.energypsych.org*
- *Science of Mind* – "The Science of Mind is the study of Life and the nature of the laws of thought; the conception that we live in a spiritual Universe; that God is in, through, around and for us." – *Dr. Ernest Holmes* – *www.religiousscience.org*
- *Siddha Yoga* – "Siddha Yoga is a spiritual path of discipline, of mastering the mind and senses with teachings and practices. It is also a path imbued with grace. Siddha Yoga practice and study is guided by meditation master and teacher Gurumayi Chidvilasananda. Gurumayi, the spiritual head of the Siddha Yoga path, teaches students to live in the awareness of the inner Self so that they can transform themselves as well as the world in which they live." (excerpt from website) *www.siddhayoga.org*
- *Unity* – "Unity was founded in 1889 in Kansas City, Missouri, by Charles and Myrtle Fillmore. After Mrs. Fillmore's remarkable healing using prayer and affirmations, many friends became interested in how she

accomplished this healing. Unity grew from small prayer circles in living rooms to the worldwide movement it is today." — *Unity Online – www.unityonline.org*

Energy Healing Resources

- Dynamic Energetic Healing (DEH)
  www.onedynamicenergetichealing.org
  www.dynamicenergetichealing.com
- Emotional Freedom Techniques (EFT)
  www.emofree.com
- Yuen Method
  www.yuenmethod.com
- Resonance Re-patterning
  www.resonancerepatterning.net/content

Movies

- *The Secret* by Rhonda Byrne. This DVD offers an educational and inspirational overview of the Law of Attraction and how to harness its power to create the life you desire.
- *What the Bleep Do We Know!?* – Starring Marlee Matlin, this cutting edge, one of a kind movie offers an entertaining and educational exploration of how the Universe works. Part narrative, part documentary, it's a 'must see' for anyone with the slightest curiosity about how we create our own realities.

About the Author

Sonia Miller's work was born out of her deep passion for seeing people overcome the obstacles that can arise when pursuing one's dreams. She founded www.SuccessForTheSoul.com, a virtual resource center visited by countless seekers all over the world, as a way to help others create the changes that lead to success, healing and transformation. Her approach uniquely blends the metaphysical principles that are the basis of all success with concrete tools for personal achievement.

Since 1989 Sonia has cultivated her expertise through her training and experience in business management, self-actualization, therapeutic applications, relationships, spirituality, metaphysics and energetic bodywork. She has worked as a counselor, coach and teacher since 1995 and holds a Bachelors Degree in Business Administration and a Masters Degree in Social Work.

Sonia joyfully expresses her purpose as a wife, mother, international life-coach, counselor, teacher, and author.

SUCCESS for the SOUL

My Gifts to You!

Free Prosperity Teleclass Audio Recording
"How to Manifest Prosperity with the Law of Attraction:
5 Must-Have Mind-Sets"

Free Subscription to "Sonia Miller's Soul Food Ezine"
Receive bi-weekly success tools by email.
Includes articles, tips, success stories, recommended
resources and more.

Free Special Report
"How to Unleash the Magic When the Law of Attraction
DOESN'T Work for You!"
Discover the top 5 blocks and breakthroughs.

To receive your gifts, go to: www.SuccessForTheSoul.com
and submit your name and email in the box that reads
"Get Everything You Want from Life!"
Once you confirm your subscription, your materials
will arrive via email shortly thereafter.

Other Learning Products by Sonia M. Miller

Harness the Power of the Law of Attraction by Getting Out of Your Own Way
Audio Program

Discover the Top 10 Ways That We Get in Our Own Way and the Mind-Set Shifts that Unleash Infinite Possibilities in Your Life!

The Vision Workshop Workbook

A Step-by-Step Guide to Knowing and Magnetizing What You Really Want!

QUICK ORDER FORM

Fax orders: 815-717-7398. Send this form.
Telephone orders: 503-961-1228
Internet orders: Go to our online store at www.successforthesoul.com.
Postal Orders: ALMA Publishing, Inc..
170 W. Ellendale, Suite 103 - #135, Dallas, OR 97338

Please send the following books or programs. I understand that I may
return any of them for a full refund – for any reason, no questions asked.

_____

_____

_____

Please send more FREE information regarding:
        ❑   Other books and information products
        ❑   Live events: speaking and classes
        ❑   Virtual events: internet classes and tele-seminars

Name:_____

Address:_____

City:_____State:_____Zip:_____

Email address:_____

Shipping and Handling:
Within the U.S. – Please add $4.00 for first book and $2.00 for each additional one. For other products, please call or email for information regarding shipping and handling charges.
Outside of the U.S. - $9.00 for first book and $5.00 for each additional
one (estimate).

Payment:
Select   ❑ Check   ❑ Money order   ❑ Credit card:
❑ Visa   ❑ MasterCard   ❑ AMEX   ❑ Discover
(Check payable to Alma Publishing, Inc.)

Card number: _____

Name on card: _____

Exp. Date: _____ Security Code: _____
(Security Code is the last 3 digits of the number on the back of the card)

CPSIA information can be obtained at www.ICGtesting.com
Printed in the USA
BVOW031316200112

280811BV00005B/2/P